THE TOP TEN
MIDDLEWEIGHT CHAMPIONS
OF ALL TIME

WHO WAS THE GREATEST?

By
Larry Carli

The Top Ten Middleweight Champions of All Time

© 2017 Larry Carli

ISBN: 978-1-61170-255-2

Published by:

Rp **Robertson Publishing**™
www.RobertsonPublishing.com

Printed in the USA and UK on acid-free paper.
To purchase additional prints of this book go to:

   amazon.com
   barnesandnoble.com

Foreword

Who was the greatest middleweight champion of all time? Was it Sugar Ray Robinson, who is frequently described as pound-for-pound the greatest fighter of all time? Was it Harry Greb who had close to 300 fights and fought while blind in one eye? Could it have been Carlos Monzon who went undefeated in fifteen world title fights? Or maybe was it Bernard Hopkins who holds the record for the longest title reign and most successful title defenses. Controversy, after all, is what boxing has always thrived upon.

This book is the author's opinion and ranking of the ten greatest middleweight champions plus a section on six great fighters who never received an opportunity to fight for a title. The book was written to be fun to read and to allow the reader an opportunity to compare his or her picks for the greatest fighters in the middleweight division.

Table of Contents

Nino Benvenuti

Photograph from Boxing Scene, April 1985

Chapter One   No. 10 Nino Benvenuti

The Italian Playboy

Giovanni "Nino" Benvenuti was born on April 26th, 1938, in the seaport city of Izola, Slovenia, and grew up in Trieste, Italy. Nino had four brothers and one sister. Unlike many other fighters, Nino was born into a middle class family and took up boxing as a hobby as a teenager. His father Fernando was a fisherman and took him to a local gym where the local amateur coaches were amazed at his hand speed and natural athletic talent.

Nino was quick to learn the basics of boxing and ripped through his opponents like a tornado. At the age of 19 in 1957 he won the European amateur welterweight title in Prague and re-peated as amateur welterweight champion in 1959 in Lucerne, while serving two years in the Italian army.

Entering the 1960 Olympics in Rome, Nino had been a five time Italian amateur boxing champion in the welterweight division and light middleweight division. Nino became an Italian national hero when he defeated Russian Yury Radonyak for the gold medal in the welterweight division.

Nino also beat out Muhammed Ali, then known as Cassius Clay, for the best boxer award in the Olympics. Ali had won Olympic gold in the light heavyweight division. The handsome and stylish Nino finished his career with an amateur record of 120 wins with no losses, or 120 wins with one loss, depending upon which boxing source is relied upon.

Nino turned professional in 1961 under the watchful eye of trainer Libero Golinelli and famed boxing manager Bruno Amaduzzi. Carefully matched in Italy by his management, Nino won his first thirty professional fights including an 11th round knockout of Tommaso Truppi for the Italian middleweight title.

Nino first entered the top ten rankings of the world Super Welterweight division when he outpointed former world champion Denny Moyer in 1964. After stretching his unbeaten streak to fifty-five he was matched with fellow Italian and world super welter-weight champion Sandro Mazzinghi in June of 1965 in Milan, Italy.

Mazzinghi was from the Tuscany area of Italy, and the whole country wanted to see this match. Mazzinghi had won the title from Ralph Dupas in 1963 and had defended his title twice. Mazzinghi was a strong puncher and Italy was equally divided on who was the better fighter.

In a thrilling evenly matched contest Nino broke loose in the 6th round and knocked out Mazzinghi to take the super welter-weight title. The former Olympic welterweight champion was now the super welterweight champion and undefeated in 56 fights.

Mazzinghi demanded a rematch but first Nino annexed the European Middleweight title with a 6th round knockout of Spaniard Luis Folledo. The rematch with Mazzinghi was to be fought in Rome in December. Mazzinghi told the press, and anyone who would listen, that Nino landed a lucky punch in the first fight and the result would be different in the rematch.

In the rematch Nino left no doubt as to who was the better fighter by nearly knocking Mazzinghi out in the early rounds and thoroughly dominating him to take a fifteen round decision. Nino was now the toast of Italy, as the good looking undefeated Italian fighter who could be seen driving down Rome's Via Veneto in his blood red colored Ferrari. You could not miss seeing Nino on television, as he was on most television talk shows.

In May of 1966 Nino fought for the first time outside of Italy, when he traveled to Berlin, Germany, to knock out Jupp Elze in the 14th round in defense of his European middleweight title. Nino was having problems making the super welterweight weight limit of 154 pounds, but decided to make one more defense of his title before challenging for the world middleweight title.

In June of 1966 Nino traveled to South Korea to defend his world super welterweight title to take on undefeated challenger and local boy Ki-Soo Kim. Nino had defeated Kim in the Olympic Games in Rome as an amateur in 1960 and he was not thought of as a particularly dangerous challenger to the title. Kim put up a surprisingly tough fight. Even though most boxing experts felt that Nino did just enough to win the decision in the close fight, the judges did not favor Nino and Kim was awarded a split decision victory. Both Nino's title and unbeaten streak were gone.

Nino moved up to the middleweight division on a permanent basis and reeled off six straight victories including a European middleweight title defense against Italian middleweight Pascal Di Benedetto in October of 1966. After his knockout victory over Di Benedetto, Nino became the number one contender to Emile Griffith's world middleweight title.

The American boxing public had heard very little about Nino as he had fought almost exclusively in Europe. The odds makers installed Nino as a huge underdog to take the title from Griffith. The fight was to be held in New York City and it stirred up a lot of interest with the huge Italian population of the area. Even though Nino had only lost one time in seventy-one fights, very few of the boxing experts gave him much of a chance to dethrone the former welterweight and current middleweight champion.

Nino started the fight by out jabbing the shorter Griffith in the first round and knocked him down in the second round with a right uppercut to the point of the chin. The third was a slow round with little action, but Griffith opened up in the fourth round and floored Nino with a lead right hand causing him to stumble sideways along the ropes before he hit the canvas. Nino got up and was able to avoid any further damage by the end of the round.

Nino used his left hook and right uppercut to take both the 5th and 6th rounds. Griffith came storming back with an effective body attack over the next three rounds and opened up a deep cut on Nino's nose with a wicked left hook. The doctor came into the ring to inspect Nino's wound and the fear of having the fight stopped seemed to energize him. Nino took over the fight during the second half of the 11th round and outfought Griffith for the remainder of the fight, peppering him with left jabs and hooks and right uppercuts. The crowd went wild when Nino was declared the winner and new champion by a clear unanimous decision by the judges.

Nino returned to Italy as the conquering hero. His picture was plastered all over the billboards in Rome and his name was in the sports pages on a daily basis. Nino took the summer off from boxing in order to let his nose heal from the injury sustained in the first Griffith fight.

Griffith indicated that he wished to exercise his option for a return match and the second fight was set to take place in September of 1967 at Shea Stadium in New York. Griffith trained diligently for the rematch and he was in top shape when he stepped into the ring for the fight in Shea Stadium. Nino appeared sluggish in the rematch and did not look like the same fighter who had won the title in April. Griffith appeared to out hustle him throughout the fight. The referee scored the bout a draw but the two judges voted for Griffith. Nino returned to Italy an ex-champion.

FIGHT OF THE YEAR

Nino Benvenuti regains Middleweight Title from Emile Griffith

Photograph from Boxing Illustrated, March 1969

Nino prepared for the third fight of the trilogy with Griffith by taking a ten round unanimous decision over middleweight trial horse Charley Austin in Rome in January of 1968. The stage was now set for the rubber match that was to take place in Madison Square Garden in New York in March of 1968. Nino stepped into the ring in the best shape of his career. This was the fight to decide once and for all which one was the better fighter of the two. The fight was evenly fought until Nino dropped Griffith in the middle rounds and roared home a victor as Griffith appeared to tire in the later rounds.

Nino returned to Italy again and remained busy through the year with a series of non-title fights. He stopped Jimmy Ramos in Turin, Italy, and ventured up to Canada to beat Art Hernandez in September. Nino prepped for his first title defense by winning a decision over tough Doyle Baird in Akron, Ohio, in October.

Nino made the first defense of his second reign as middle-weight champion by taking on top contender Don Fullmer in Liguria, Italy, in December. Nino had already defeated Fullmer in a non-title fight in February of 1966. Fullmer had improved dra-matically since that fight and he was the younger brother of former middleweight champion Gene Fullmer. Nino had to get off of the canvas during the fight to win a convincing unanimous decision over Fullmer.

Even though Nino was winning his fights with his slick boxing skills, it was noticed that he had been dropped in several of his recent fights. Nino began toying with the idea of taking on light heavyweights and he signed to fight former middleweight and light heavyweight champion Dick Tiger in May of 1969. Tiger gave Nino a brutal body beating in taking a ten round decision over him and sending him back to the middleweight ranks.

Nino defended his title next in October against undefeated newcomer Fraser Scott in Naples, Italy. In a strange foul-filled bout,

Scott was disqualified for "ducking low" in the 7th round. Scott was awkward and strong and the referee handled the fight like it was an amateur contest. It did not help that Scott did not understand Italian nor could he change his style of fighting.

With the Scott fiasco behind him, Nino signed to fight top contender and former welterweight champion Luis Rodriguez in Rome in November of 1969. Nino was cut badly across the bridge of his nose and appeared to be losing the fight when he connected with a perfect left hook to Rodriguez's head in the 11th round to win by knockout.

In March of 1970 Nino ventured to Australia to take on middleweight Tom "The Bomb" Bethea in a ten round non-title bout. Bethea surprised everyone by stopping Nino with a body attack in the 8th round. It appeared that Nino was making a habit of losing non-title fights. Nino decided to give Bethea a title fight and this time he knocked out Bethea in the same 8th round in Umago, Italy, two months later in May.

Nino took on old foe Doyle Baird in a non-title fight in Bari, Italy, in September. Nino knocked Baird out in the 10th round as a tune up for his world title fight against top contender Carlos Monzon.

Nino defended his title against the little known Argentine in November of 1970, in Rome, Italy. It appeared right from the start of the fight that Monzon was just too strong for Nino. Nino made a valiant effort to defend his title but Monzon caught him with a perfect right hand along the ropes in the 12th round. Nino dropped to the canvas heavily and when he got up he was in no condition to continue the fight as he fell into the ropes. Monzon stunned the Italian fans and the world with his knockout victory. Many boxing fans felt that Nino just had an off night but he did not look good in tuning up for the Monzon rematch by dropping a decision to Argentine Jose Chirino in March of 1971.

The Monzon rematch took place in May of 1971 in Monte Carlo. The rematch was strictly one sided as Nino's corner threw in the towel in the 3rd round to save him from further punishment. Nino protested the stoppage, but it appeared that he had no chance of winning the fight when it was stopped. This proved to be the last fight of Nino's long and successful ring career.

Nino had a great boxing career. He was an Olympic gold medalist, a onetime super welterweight, and a two time world middleweight champion as a professional. I would consider Nino as probably the greatest fighter to ever come out of Italy. He may also arguably be the best middleweight champion during the decade of the 1960's.

As noted by writer Jim Amato, Nino was not in the mold of aggressive former Italian-American champions such as Rocky Marciano, Rocky Graziano, and Carmen Basilio. Nino was a slick boxer with fast hands and an elegant style of boxing. His suave and debonair personality matched his boxing skills in the ring. Though not noted as a knockout artist, Nino had a decent left hook, and right uppercut which made opponents respect him in the ring.

Upon retirement, Nino became a sportscaster in Italy and even had his own show at one time on Italian television. He was a very successful businessman in his hometown of Trieste and actually served on a city council.

Nino was known as a great humanitarian as he worked with Mother Theresa helping the needy and was known to help former opponents Emile Griffith and Carlos Monzon in time of need. He helped Griffith out financially after his retirement and he visited Monzon regularly when he was in jail in Argentina in the 1990's.

Nino's final ring record was 82 wins, 7 losses, and 1 draw. He scored 35 knockouts. As of this writing Nino is alive and well, living in Trieste, Italy. Nino was inducted into the International Boxing Hall of Fame in 1990.

Tony Zale

Photograph from Boxing Illustrated, September 1965

Chapter Two   No. 9 Tony Zale

The Man of Steel

There was never a more rugged competitor in the middle-weight division then the man born Anthony Florian Zaleski on May 29, 1913, in Gary, Indiana, to a Polish immigrant family. Besides his strong body punching, he was also known for his grim determination and remarkable recuperative powers in the ring.

Tony entered the Golden Gloves in 1931 and was the Indiana state champion in the lightweight division. In 1932 he lost in the finals in the welterweight division of the Golden Gloves tournament held in Chicago. As an amateur he won 87 out of 95 fights with 50 wins coming by knockout. There was no money fighting as an amateur during the Great Depression, so Tony turned professional in 1934 and was managed by his brother John. Tony racked up nine straight wins before losing a decision to Billy Hood in August of 1934. After the Hood fight, Tony fought twelve more times during the year, losing roughly half of his fights. Fighting out of Chicago in 1935, Tony did not fare much better losing three of his seven fights.

Tony had only one fight in 1936 fighting a draw with Jack Moran. Part of the reason for Tony's losses and inactivity was because he had to work in the Gary, Indiana, steel mills to support himself and he needed time to recover from some boxing injuries.

Finally in 1937 Tony decided to dedicate all of his time to his boxing career. He won six of seven fights, splitting a pair of decisions with highly regarded Nate Bolden. The big change in Tony's career was hooking up with managers Sam Pain and Art Winch. Under the new management team he defeated Bolden again in a rematch to start off 1938 and he won eight of eleven fights with two losses and one draw during the year. That year he suffered a knockout at the hands of Jimmy Clark in February and in June Tony returned the favor by knocking Clark out in a rematch.

Tony started off 1939 by losing a decision to old foe Nate Bolden but he finished the year with seven straight wins with six of the victories coming by knockout. Tony was becoming a fan favorite in Chicago with his aggressive slam bang style of fighting and he appeared to get better as the quality of his completion improved.

Finally in January of 1940 Tony's management team made an offer for National Boxing Association middleweight champion Al Hostak to come to Chicago to fight Tony in a ten round non-title fight. Hostak did not know much about Tony and took him lightly coming into the fight. Hostak dropped Tony in the first round and nearly knocked him out. Hostak went all out for the knockout in the first five rounds and punched himself out. Hostak injured a hand in the middle of the fight and Tony come on strong over the second half of the fight to take the decision. Most boxers would have been unable to survive the punches that Hostak laid on Tony in the first round but Tony could definitely take a punch and came back to win the fight.

Tony had been promised a shot at Hostak's title if he won the non-title match in Chicago. Tony won his next three fights by knockout fighting out of the Chicago area before challenging Hostak to a title fight. Hostak finally agreed to put his title on the line in July of 1940 but he insisted that the fight had to take place in his hometown of Seattle. Tony agreed to the location of the fight and the bout was set for July 19th in Hostaks hometown.

The hometown advantage did not do Hostak any good as Tony proved his first win over him was no fluke and he won the title with a 13th round technical knockout. Tony was dropped by Hostak early in the fight again and survived another early barrage before he eventually wore Hostak down with a devastating body attack to stop him and take the title. As in the first fight, Hostak claimed that he broke his hand and he wanted a rematch for the title.

After having over sixty professional fights over a six year period, Tony had finally made it to the top of the middleweight division. He returned to Chicago the month after his title fight and lost a ten round decision to tall and lanky Billy Soose.

Tony felt that Seattle was his lucky town and he returned there in November to take on the ever dangerous Fred Apostoli. Apostoli was also known as a vicious body puncher and, in a no holds barred match, Tony emerged the victor with a ten round decision win.

In January of 1941, Tony took on little known Steve Mamakos from Washington D.C. in Chicago. Mamakos gave Tony a tough fight in their ten round match, but not tough enough to win the decision, and Tony rewarded him with a title fight in February. The title fight was to be held in Chicago and this time Mamakos was leading on the scorecards going into the 13th round. Just when it appeared that Tony was going to lose a decision, he cut loose with everything he had to knock Mamakos down at the end of the round. Mamakos had not recovered from the knockdown at the end of the 13th round and Tony stopped him in just seconds into the 14th round. In May, Tony returned to Chicago to stop Hostak in two rounds to end their three bout series.

Tony was the National Boxing Association middleweight champion but he did not have universal recognition as champion when he signed to fight top contender Georgie Abrams in New

York City in November of 1941. Abrams was a classy boxer who had defeated top contender Billy Soose three times to earn his shot at the world title.

Tony got off to his usual slow start and was dropped by Abrams in the very first round. During the early going of the fight Abrams suffered a severe cut eye which hampered him throughout the fight. The fight escalated into a full-fledged give and take war with Abrams holding his own throughout the first half of the fight. Tony was the stronger of the two fighters and landed the harder punches during the second half of the fight. Abrams fought hard until the end of the fight but Tony was awarded the championship on a close but unanimous fifteen round decision.

The following month the United States was at war after the Japanese attack on Pearl Harbor. Tony joined the Navy and fought a twelve round non-title fight with Billy Conn before his title was frozen during the duration of the war years. Conn, who was a light heavyweight, proved to be a little too big for Tony and Conn took the twelve round decision.

During the war years, while Tony was in the Navy, Rocky Graziano was making a name for himself in the New York area with his deadly punching power. Though Rocky was not much of a boxer, he could knock anyone out early or late in a fight with his straight right hand punch.

Graziano eagerly awaited Tony's return from the service to get him into the ring in a fight for the title. Tony got out of the service at the end of the war and got into shape by scoring knockouts in six non-title fights. The title fight was to be held in New York City in September of 1946. Tony was 33 years old at the time and some boxing experts felt that Tony was passed his prime for this fight.

Tony Zale batters Rocky Graziano into the ropes

Photograph from Boxing & Wrestling Magazine, January 1962

The fight began with Graziano tearing into Tony with everything he had and staggered Tony in every round. By the end of the 5th round the referee went to Tony's corner and asked him if he wanted to continue the fight. During the 6th round Tony doubled

15

up Graziano with a body shot and a left hook to the head and dropped Graziano to the mat. Graziano made a vain attempt to get up but he just missed beating the ten count.

Tony made one of the greatest comebacks in history as he was on the verge of getting knocked out several times before he put Graziano away for good. Tony was named fighter of the year by Ring magazine and the fight with Graziano was named the fight of the year for 1946.

Tony took four months from boxing to recover from his injuries before entering the ring again in February of 1947. Tony won all five of his tune up fights by knockout before his rematch with Graziano. The rematch was scheduled for July and it was to be held in Tony's adopted hometown of Chicago.

The roles were reversed in this fight, as it was Tony who got off to a fast start by cutting Graziano and battering him all over the ring for the first five rounds. Graziano came out for the 6th round knowing that he was badly cut and that the fight was close to being stopped by the referee. Graziano went wild with non-stop lefts and rights to Tony's head. Tony sagged against the ropes defenseless as the referee pulled the enraged Graziano off of him and stopped the fight. Graziano was now the new middleweight champion of the world and Tony was a 34 year old ex-champ. Tony's fight with Graziano was again named the fight of the year by Ring magazine for 1947.

Tony took six months off from the ring again and got back to work by winning all three tune-up fights while waiting for the third fight in the trilogy with Graziano. The third fight was to take place in Newark, New Jersey, in June of 1948. Tony trained hard to get his by now 35 year old body in shape for the contest.

The third contest was not as evenly fought as the first two contests. Graziano did stagger Tony once in the early rounds before

Tony landed a picture perfect left hook to Graziano's head to knock him out cold in the third round. Graziano's head literally bounced off of the canvas a couple of times when he went down.

Tony's wars with Graziano were probably the most famous middleweight rivalry in middleweight history. It just seemed that Tony was getting better with age and could go on forever. Tony defended his title for the last time against Frenchmen Marcel Cerdan in September in Jersey City. In this fight it seemed that Tony just got old all of a sudden as he was never really seriously in the fight. Tony did hurt Cerdan once in an early round with a body shot but Cerdan gave him a systematic beating until Tony collapsed along the ropes into the referee's arms at the end of the 11th round. Tony was physically spent and could not come out for the 12th round. Cerdan was the new champion and Tony went out on his shield as he had given the fight everything that he had.

After fourteen hard years in the ring, Tony decided to retire. He had offers to fight Cerdan in a rematch but Tony was smart enough to know that his time had come to leave the ring. Tony returned to his hometown of Chicago and spent his retirement years giving back to the community by coaching the Catholic Youth Organization's boxing teams.

With his dignified and quiet personality, he remained admired by boxing fans all over the world. Tony was a fighter who gave it his all in the ring and could truly be called a credit to the sport of boxing.

Tony retired with a ring record of 67 wins, 18 losses, and 2 draws. He won 45 fights by knockout. He was inducted into the International Boxing Hall of Fame in 1991. Tony passed away at the age of 83 in 1997.

Marcel Cerdan

Photograph from International Boxing, February 1973

Chapter Three   No. 8 Marcel Cerdan

The Tiger of Casablanca

Marcel Cerdan was born Marcellin Cerdan on July 22, 1916, in Algeria. He was born into a fighting family as his father, Emile, and older brothers, Vincent and Armand, had been fighters. Therefore it was decided at an early age, by his father, that Marcel would also become a boxer.

At the age of 16 Marcel met Lucian Roupp. Roupp ran a garage in Casablanca and was involved in the boxing business. This would be the beginning of a lifelong relationship between fighter and manager.

Marcel turned professional in 1934 at the age of 18 and won thirty straight professional fights under Roupp's management before taking the French welterweight title from Omar Kouidri in February of 1938 in Casablanca. Marcel defeated Kouidri in a rematch for the French title in Paris in November.

Marcel continued unbeaten in his first forty-six professional fights before he fought Englishman Henry Craster in London in January of 1939. The British referee felt that Marcels body punches were too low and he disqualified Marcel in the fifth round of a fight he was easily winning.

Six weeks after the Craster fight Marcel defeated world ranked Saverio Turiello by decision in Paris. In June of 1939, Marcel traveled to Milan, Italy, to take the European Welterweight title from Turiello in a rematch.

Marcel did not fight in 1940 as he joined the French army during World War II. Marcel remained unbeaten in 1941 as he fought mainly in Algiers and Casablanca. During the Nazi occupation Marcel returned to the mainland. In 1942 and 1943, Marcel fought a total of fourteen times with just one loss on a foul to Victor Buttin in August of 1942 in Algiers. In 1944, Marcel knocked out Joe DiMartino in one round to win the Inter-Allied Middleweight championship.

When the war ended in 1945, Marcel traveled to Paris in November to win the French middleweight title from Assane Dioui. The following month Marcel avenged his disqualification loss to Victor Buttin by knocking him out in three rounds in St. Etienne. In July of 1946, Marcel got the attention of the American boxing public by beating world ranked Holman Williams in ten rounds in Paris. French promoter Jo Longman began making preparations for Marcel to invade New York and test his skills against the world's greatest middleweights. Marcels American debut was to take place in December against top ranked middleweight Georgie Abrams in New York City.

Marcel proved that he belonged in the top ten of the world middleweight rankings by taking a highly competitive ten round decision over the always tough and clever Abrams. Even though Abrams survived and made the fight competitive, there was no doubt that Marcel had a clear advantage in the fight.

In February of 1947, Marcel returned to Paris to knock out Leon Fouquet in one round for the European middleweight title. Marcel returned to New York City to dismantle the talented Harold Green in two rounds and in October he signed to fight the always tough veteran Anton Raadik in Chicago.

Marcel Cerdan bangs a right hand to the head of a bloody Georgie Abrams

Photograph from International Boxing, February 1973

Marcel started off fast in the Raadik fight and was winning most of the rounds and it appeared he was on his way to winning an easy decision. It seemed like Marcel ran out of gas in the 10th round and Raadik dropped him three times and only the final bell saved him from a knockout. Marcel was given the decision but it appeared that he was not ready for a title fight at this time. Marcel would later claim that he had been sick going into the fight and he did not pace himself properly in his weakened condition.

Marcel returned to France in January of 1948 and he knocked out Giovanni Manca in two rounds to defend his European Middleweight title. Marcel was back in New York in May and he never looked better then when he stopped the very popular LaVerne Roach in eight rounds.

In May, Marcel defended his European middleweight title against cagey veteran Cyrill Delannoit in Brussels. The veteran Delannoit surprised Marcel and won a fifteen round decision over him to take his European middleweight title. This is one of only two fights that Marcel would really lose in his career as his disqualification losses could easily be discounted.

In July, Marcel returned to Brussels to challenge Delannoit for the European middleweight title. This fight was also a title eliminator with the winner to challenge champion Tony Zale for the world middleweight title. Marcel was a crafty veteran at this point in his career and he decisively beat Delannoit to win back his European title and get a title fight against Zale.

The date for Marcel's title fight was set for September 21, 1948, in Jersey City. Zale had been fresh off of a knockout victory over Rocky Graziano in June and it was largely felt that he would be too rugged for Marcel. Zale seemed to be improving with age and did not appear to be slowing down at all.

Marcel had a good training camp and he stepped into the ring in Jersey City in top physical shape. Zale was always in top condition so this figured to be an all-out war between two aggressive body punchers.

Zale started out strong and it appeared like he seemed to want to end the fight quickly as he went for the knockout in several of the early rounds. Marcel was pacing himself and was exchanging vicious body shots with the champion. As the rounds wore on it appeared that Zale was getting weaker and Marcel was getting stronger. By the 9th round it appeared to all that Zale was just fighting to go out a champion and his punches carried no power. Marcel increased his body attack as Zale began to fade rapidly. Near the end of the 11th round, Marcel leaped in with a left hook to Zale's head. As the bell rang to end the round, Zale sunk to his knees and into the arms of the referee. Zale was unable to come out for the 12ᵗʰ round and Marcel was middleweight champion of the whole world. Marcel celebrated in the middle of the ring with Lucien Roupp and Jo Longman. Famed French singer, Edith Piaf, celebrated in the audience as did the whole nation of France.

The "The Tiger of Casablanca" boxed a couple of exhibition matches in the United States before coming home to an adoring French public. Marcel scored knockouts in a couple of tune up fights in March and in May in preparation for his first title defense against '"The Raging Bull" Jake LaMotta. His title defense against Lamotta was to take place in June of 1949, in Detroit. LaMotta was the only fighter that had defeated Sugar Ray Robinson up to that time and he had been a top contender in the division for over five years. After all the years of trying to get a title fight, LaMotta was determined not to let this opportunity to win the title pass him by.

LaMotta came out aggressively in the first round and Marcel fell to the canvas hard from what appeared to be a combination punch and shove. Marcel was up immediately and fighting back. As the early rounds wore on, it was apparent that something was wrong as Marcel began fighting back one handed. Marcel had ap-parently injured his left shoulder when he fell to the canvas in the first round and he was unable to use it as the rounds passed by. By the 10ᵗʰ round Marcel was unable to hold LaMotta off with one arm and he was unable to come out of his corner to continue the battle. LaMotta had finally achieved the title that he had sought for years but there was no doubt due to Marcel's injury that Marcel deserved a rematch for the title.

Marcel returned to France determined to regain his title that he felt had lost due to injury. He trained hard for the rematch and his shoulder was totally healed. He was set to fly to the United States for the rematch when word came out from LaMottas camp that he had been injured in training. Marcel waited patiently while LaMotta healed and when the rematch was set he boarded a plane from France to the United States.

23

Fate would intervene as Marcel and all the passengers aboard his plane died when their plane crashed into a mountain in the Azores on October 27th, 1949. At the age of 33 the former middleweight champion and idol of France was dead. Shock waves were felt in France as people could not believe what had happened. Marcel appeared indestructible to the people of France and now their hero was dead.

Many boxing experts felt that Marcel would have defeated LaMotta in the rematch but this is something that no one would ever know. France mourned as Marcel was laid to rest amongst tributes from the boxing fraternity around the world.

No one would ever see the chunky, hairy chested brawler, who punched with pin point accuracy, ever fight again. His amiable nature made him a fan favorite around the world. His ruggedness and tenacity were admired by the boxing public. No one would ever know just how great he could have been.

Most boxing experts have placed Marcel in the top ten of all time middleweight champions. Even though Georges Carpentier was the first French boxing hero from the 1920's, I believe that Marcel was a better all-around fighter and the best fighter to ever come out of France. He had with an outstanding ring record of 111 wins and with just 4 losses, of which 2 losses were by disqualification. He won 65 fights by knockout. He was inducted into the International Boxing Hall of Fame in 1991.

Bob Fitzsimmons

Photograph from the Big Book of Boxing, March 1983

Chapter Four   No. 7 Bob Fitzsimmons

Ruby Robert

Bob Fitzsimmons was probably the hardest puncher of all the middleweight champions. He was the first middleweight champion to win the light heavyweight and heavyweight championships. He was also the only middleweight champion to hold all three titles as I do not consider Roy Jones victory over John Ruiz as a heavyweight championship bout.

Robert James "Bob" Fitzsimmons was born on May 26th in 1863, in Cornwall, England. When he was nine years old his family migrated to Helston on the east coast of New Zealand's south island. Bob was an outstanding sprinter and soccer player in school and, at an early age, he was apprenticed to a blacksmith. Bob developed tremendous shoulder and arm strength by pounding a sledgehammer on an anvil to shape sections of iron.

At the age of 17, Bob had a meeting with famous bareknuckle fighter Jem Mace who took one look at his broad shoulders and encouraged him to fight in his sponsored amateur tournaments. At the age of 18, Bob won an amateur tournament sponsored by Mace when he defeated four different opponents. Bob repeated as tournament champion in 1881 by defeating five different men. At a body weight of around 150 pounds Bob became the amateur Heavyweight boxing champion of New Zealand.

Bob traveled to Sydney, Australia, in a two masted schooner to begin his professional boxing career. Some sources reported that he entered the paid ranks when he defeated Jim Crawford in 1883 while modern day statistics show that he turned professional when he decisioned Joe Riddle in 1885.

Mace trained Bob to utilize his strength by throwing short compact punches to the body and head. Under Mace's guidance Bob developed his famous "solar plexus" punch to the body that, when delivered properly, would temporarily paralyze opponents.

Bob learned his trade fighting some of Australia's best fighters from 1885 to 1890. With a record of 16 wins and just 2 losses and 2 draws, Bob sailed to San Francisco, California, to exchange blows with some of the best middleweights in the business.

Bob stood nearly 6 feet tall, weighed around 158 pounds, had broad shoulders, and spindly legs. Bob was also heavily freckled and he did not look like a stereotype fighter when he arrived at San Francisco's athletic club.

Bob was immediately matched with the clubs top middleweight Frank Allen in May of 1890. Bob removed any doubt that he could punch as he knocked Allen cold in the very first round. Athletic club officials thought that Bob's win was a fluke and he was then matched with the more experienced Billy McCarthy ten days after the Allen fight. McCarthy made the mistake at poking fun at Bob's physical appearance before the fight. Bob decided to give McCarthy a real beating for insulting him and eventually knocked him out in the 5th round. Everyone was now convinced that Bob was a legitimate contender for the world middleweight title.

Bob went to New Orleans, Louisiana, to fight an elimination fight for the middleweight title. In July Bob was matched with Arthur Upton with the winner to get a title fight with the champion

Nonpareil Jack Dempsey. Spectators were astonished at Bob's power when he knocked Upton out in nine rounds.

In January of 1891, Bob returned to New Orleans to challenge Dempsey at the Olympic club to a fight for the middleweight title. Dempsey whose real name was John Kelly was born in Ireland and had migrated to New York in 1880. Dempsey had fought with bare knuckles and with gloves in his career. From 1883 to 1888, Dempsey had been undefeated in 55 fights. Everyone thought that Dempsey would be too crafty for Bob and he was a huge favorite to win at fight time.

Once again Bob proved the experts wrong as he floored Dempsey a total of thirteen times before mercifully knocking him out in the 13th round. Dempsey fell face forward to the ground after the last knockdown and the slaughter finally stopped. The last blow of the fight was a crushing right hand to Dempsey's Adams Apple.

As there was no money at the time in fighting middleweights, Bob turned his attention to the Heavyweight division. Bob had the same success in the heavyweight division as he did in the middleweight division. As there was no light heavyweight division at the time, Bob had to give away up to 40 pounds to his heavyweight opponents.

Bob's first impressive victory as a heavyweight was when he knocked out top contender Peter Maher in twelve rounds in March of 1892. At a body weight of approximately 165 pounds, Bob continued to knock out heavyweights and was eventually matched with perennial top contender Joe Choynski. The match was supposed to be a five round exhibition match in Boston in June of 1894. The match did start out as an exhibition until Choynski dropped Bob with a solid punch. Bob recovered quickly and retaliated with a furious attack that had Choynski reeling around the ring until the police broke up the fight.

29

In September of 1894, Bob returned to New Orleans to make a defense of his middleweight title before turning his total attention to the heavyweight division. Bob easily knocked out Dan Creedon in two rounds in the one and only defense of his middleweight title. Though he made no more defenses of his title he was still generally recognized as middleweight champion up until 1897.

Under the guidance of new manager, Mitchell Julian, Bob campaigned for a shot at the heavyweight title held by Jim Corbett. Corbett won the title in 1892 from John L. Sullivan and had defended it one time; defeating 155 pound Charley Mitchell in 1894.

In February of 1896 Bob strengthened his qualifications for a title shot by knocking out Ireland's Peter Maher again. This time Bob knocked out the Irishman in the very first round. This victory set up a match with Sailor Tom Sharkey with the winner to challenge Corbett for the title.

In December of 1896, Bob took on the tough Sailor in San Francisco, California, in a ten round fight. Bob was getting the best of Sharkey and had survived all of his lethal blows through the first seven rounds. In the 8th round, Bob landed his "solar plexus" punch and Sharkey fell to the ground clutching his groin and screaming that he had been fouled. No one in the whole audience saw the foul, but referee Wyatt Earp still disqualified Bob and awarded the match to Sharkey. Rumors were floated about that Earp had bet money on Sharkey, but this was never proven.

Without any doubt that Bob was the most deserving of the title challengers, Corbett eventually agreed to defend his heavyweight title against him in March of 1897 in Carson City, Nevada. There was huge interest in this fight as it was well known that Bob and Corbett had a mutual dislike for each other. Bob fought an exhibition match with Ernest Roeber in January. Bob knocked out poor Roeber in the very first round - as even exhibitions could turn into a serious match.

Jim Corbett was a slick boxer with fast hands and great footwork. Many of the boxing experts felt that Corbett would out-box Bob to gain a decision win. This bout was to be the first heavyweight title fight ever to be filmed. Bob weighed in at 167 pounds for the fight and Corbett came in at 183 pounds. Corbett was also the slightly taller of the two. This match was advertised in the newspapers as "The battle of the century" and news reporters came to Carson City from all around the United States to report on the fight.

Both fighters entered the ring and the spectators got their first look at the freakish looking Fitzsimmons. Bob had the upper body of a heavyweight and, with his spindly legs, the lower body of a bantamweight. Corbett on the other hand was evenly proportioned and was always dapper looking in the ring.

Corbett started off the bout fast, hooking and jabbing with his left hand and making a bloody mess of Bob's face. Bob went down in the 6th round but with his amazing recuperative powers he was up and fought on even terms in the 7th round. It appeared to the fans at ringside that Corbett was slowing down from the fast pace that he set in the fight and that Bob was gaining strength as the bout progressed.

Though his face was a bloody mess, Bob began reaching Corbett around the 12th round with some of his power shots. Finally, in the 14th round, Bob saw the moment he was waiting for in the whole fight. Bob observed for a moment that Corbett had left his body unprotected and he drove a hard left into the solar plexus of Corbett. Corbett appeared shocked as he slowly sank to the canvas. Corbett crawled around the canvas on his hands and knees and made a vain attempt to grab the ropes and pull himself up at the count of ten. Corbett failed to beat the count and Bob was proclaimed the new heavyweight champion.

When Corbett got up and realized what happened, he was enraged and wanted to continue the fight. His handlers had to keep him from attacking Bob after the fight. Bob would never give Corbett a rematch for the title. Later Corbett lost two fights by knockout trying to regain the title from Jim Jeffries before he retired from the ring.

Bob Fitzsimmons wins title from Jim Corbett

Photograph from Big Book of Boxing, March 1983

Bob stated after the fight, that he drew incentive to continue the fight after he was knocked down when he heard his wife Rose from ringside hollering to him to hit Corbett in the "slats" (ribs). The balding freakish looking 167 pounder, who would fight in the super middleweight division of today, was now the heavyweight champion of the whole world.

In June Bob traveled to Leadville, Colorado, to knock out an unfortunate fighter named Lew Joslin in the 2nd round of a four round exhibition match. After the exhibition match, Bob did what most heavyweight champions of his day did and that was to use to their celebrity to make money in the theatre. Bob took 1898 off from boxing and traveled across the United States giving audiences displays of his prowess as a blacksmith. Bob's wife Rose, who happened to be his manager Mitchell Julian's sister, traveled with him. Bob did not fight again until he chose to defend his title against a much bigger and stronger opponent named James J. Jeffries.

Jeffries was nicknamed "The Boilermaker" due to the trade he had prior to his ring career. Like Bob, it was a trade that helped harden the muscles on his 6 foot 2 inch, 220 pound frame. Even though Jeffries had a huge size advantage on Bob, he was not expected to take the title due to his relative crudeness in the ring. Most experts felt that Bob would box circles around the big man and then knock him out. Jeffries had been one of Jim Corbett's sparring partners for his fight with Bob and he fought out of a crouch, which made him a difficult target to hit inside the ring.

The title fight was set for June 8, 1899, and was to take place in Coney Island, New York. Bob weighed in at 167 pounds and Jeffries had slimmed down to 206 pounds for the contest. Bob came out cautiously and found Jeffries a difficult target to hit inside of his crouch. When Bob did land his punches on Jeffries they seemed to have no real effect.

Bob landed blows on Jefferies' head that would have knocked most heavyweights out but Jeffries would just shake off the blows and keep plodding forward. Though Bob could punch like a heavyweight, his body could not withstand the power of Jeffries blows. Jeffries wore Bob down and eventually knocked him out with a left hook to the head and a right uppercut to the point of the chin in the 11th round. Bob could just not overcome the size difference in the match.

Bob returned to Coney Island in 1900 and scored a couple of knockouts that earned him a rematch with Jeffries. On August 10th he knocked out the top ten contender Gus Ruhlin in six rounds and knocked out old foe Tom Sharkey in two rounds.

Bob had to wait until July in 1902 to get Jeffries back into the ring with him. Jeffries had decisioned Tom Sharkey and knocked out former champion Jim Corbett in defense of his title. In the re-match Bob weighed 172 pounds to Jeffries 219.

Bob started out fast and was slashing Jeffries face to ribbons. Bob closed Jeffries left eye and, by today's standards, the fight would have been stopped. Jeffries came out desperate in the 8th round and cornered Bob and knocked him out with a vicious left to the liver. Bob was unable to beat the ten count and Jeffries had re-tained his title.

Bob returned to the ring in November of 1903 and won the newly formed light heavyweight title with a twenty round decision over George Gardner. This win made Bob the first fighter in history to win three world titles. Bob would lose his title to Philadelphia Jack O'Brien and would continue fighting until past the age of 60. Bob had his final bout in 1914.

Bob would go down in the history as the first man to hold world titles in three different weight divisions. Bob was probably pound for pound one of the hardest punchers in the history of boxing. His final ring record was 61 wins, 8 losses, and 4 draws. He won 57 fights by knockout. Bob's record in newspaper decisions was 7 wins, 4 losses, 9 draws, and 7 no decisions.

Due to several divorces and bad business investments Bob died, basically, financially destitute on October 22, 1917, in Chicago, Illinois. Bob was inducted into the International Boxing Hall of Fame in the Old Timers category in 1990.

Marvin Hagler

Photograph from Boxing Beat, September 1987

Chapter Five   No. 6 Marvin Hagler

Marvelous Marvin

Marvin Hagler was born on May 23, 1954 in Newark, New Jersey. His mother moved the family to Brockton, Massachusetts, to escape the violence at the time in Newark. Marvin gained a interest in boxing and became involved with Pat and Goody Petronelli as he entered the amateur ranks.

Under the guidance of the Petronelli brothers Marvin lost only two out of 54 amateur contests and was the 1973 National American Amateur Union middleweight boxing champion. Marvin decided he did not want to remain an amateur and wait for the 1976 Olympic trials.

Marvin turned professional on May 18th, 1973, by knocking out Terry Ryan in Brockton. Marvin was an aggressive heavy handed southpaw who reminded the people of Brockton of another heavy handed boxer from Brockton, the heavyweight named Rocky Marciano.

Marvin was carefully matched by the Petronelli brothers and moved steadily up the middleweight ranks. Marvin first gained national attention when he defeated unbeaten Olympian Sugar Ray Seales in Boston, in August of 1974. The following month Marvin gave Seales a rematch and they fought to a draw in Seales' hometown of Seattle. A draw in Seattle was equivalent to a win for Marvin had the fight taken place in any other city.

Marvin cleaned out all of his middleweight competition in the New England area and turned his attention to Philadelphia to increase his level of competition. Marvin had to become a road warrior to get fights with top opponents and he was matched with hometown popular Philadelphia fighter Bobby "Boogaloo" Watts. At the Spectrum in Philadelphia in January of 1976, Marvin was the aggressor in the fight but, after ten rounds, the judges awarded Watts a majority decision and Marvin was no longer undefeated.

Marvin returned to Philadelphia in March to fight another popular fighter in Willie "The Worm" Monroe. Monroe won a unanimous decision from Marvin. Marvin felt that this was the only fight that he truly lost in his career. It appeared in the fight that Marvin had trouble with fast stepping boxers.

Marvin returned to Philadelphia again in 1976 to stop Eugene "Cyclone" Hart and knocked out Monroe twice in 1977 to avenge his earlier defeat. In November of 1977, Mike Colbert came to the Boston Garden to do battle with Marvin. Marvin knocked Colbert out and broke his jaw in the process. Marvin was now the number one contender for the middleweight title but was unable to get a title shot.

Former European middleweight champion Kevin Finnegan, traveled to Boston in March of 1978 to take on Marvin. Marvin stopped Finnegan on cuts. Finnegan would need about forty stitches to close cuts on his face. Finnegan insisted on a rematch and Marvin again stopped the former European middleweight champ in May.

In August of 1978 Marvin traveled back to Philadelphia to take on three time middleweight title challenger Bennie Briscoe. Briscoe was known for his toughness and aggressive style of boxing. Marvin won a convincing ten round decision in the battle of the two shaved head gladiators. Neither fighter took a backward step but Marvin was just too good of a boxer for Bennie to handle.

In February of 1979 Marvin fought old foe Sugar Ray Seales. Marvin had vastly improved since their first two fights and he stopped Seales easily. In June of 1979 Marvin knocked out Argentine Norberto Cabrera on the Hugo Corro vs. Vito Anutofermo undercard. Antuofermo came on strong during the latter part of the 15 round fight and took a split decision to win the title. The stage was now set for Marvin to challenge Antuofermo for the title. The title fight was to be held in November in Las Vegas. Marvin opened up as a favorite to take the title from the scrappy Italian. This fight was to be one half of a double header featuring Wilfred Benitez vs. Sugar Ray Leonard in the other half of the main event.

Marvin started off fast, out boxing Anutofermo for the first half of the fight and looked like he should have been the favorite in the fight. The gutsy Antuofermo soaked up all of Marvin's punishment and came on strong over the middle portion of the fight. The fighters battled on even terms during the last few rounds as Antuofermo was able to back Marvin up. Most boxing experts felt that Marvin had done enough to win the decision, but Anutofermo apparently did enough in the fight to catch the judge's eyes and the verdict was a draw. A champion keeps the title with a draw decision and thus Marvin was relegated back down to being a top contender again.

Marvin rebounded in 1980 and won three straight wins including reversing one of his losses to Bobby "Boogaloo" Watts. In September, Marvin challenged new champion Alan Minter in London, England. Before the fight he was accused of not shaking hands with Minter but Marvin never shook hands with an opponent until after the fight.

The first round of the championship fight was fairly even and there was not much to choose from between the two. Marvin opened up in the second round and cut Minter around the eyes. Minter walked back to his corner battered at round's end. Marvin went all out in the third round and it seemed every time he hit Minter it opened up another cut. Finally, Minters corner threw the towel in to save their fighter from further punishment. Just as Marvin was starting to celebrate his victory the fans began throwing bottles into the ring. Marvin and his handlers had to be escorted from the stadium by the police. It appeared that the riot may have been racially related as Minter was blamed, at least partially, by the press for the riot because of some comments that he made before the fight. It was reported that Minter claimed that no black man could take the title from him.

Marvin made three defenses of his title in 1981. He stopped Fully Obelmejias in January and in June he stopped Antuofermo in a rematch. Both of the Obelmeijas and Anutofermo fights were in the Boston Garden. In October, Marvin stopped top contender Mustafa Hamsho in the Chicago area. Hamsho was tough and took a severe beating before the referee saved him in the 11th round. Hamsho took about the same amount of stitches to close cuts on his face as did Kevin Finnegan.

Marvin remained a dominant force in the middleweight division in 1982. He made quick work of William "Caveman" Lee and knocked out Fully Obelmejias in a rematch. Marvin started off 1983 by knocking out tough Englishman Tony Sibson and rugged contender Wilford Scypion. In November, Marvin had his toughest defense when he took on the legendary Roberto Duran. Duran appeared much smaller than Marvin in the ring but Duran put up a tough fight and the scorecards showed that the fight was dead even after thirteen rounds. Marvin took the last two rounds and walked away with the unanimous decision.

Most ring observers were surprised that Duran gave Marvin such a tough fight and felt that Marvin might be slipping a little bit. In March of 1984, wild swinging Argentine Juan Domingo Roldan dropped Marvin early in the fight. Roldan was putting up a good showing until he got cut and quit in the 10th round. It should be noted that Marvin's knockdown appeared to be more of a combination of a half push and slip but he still had to take the only count in his career. Roldan would say after the fight that Marvin thumbed him in the eye during the match. Marvin made quick work of Mustafa Hamsho in their rematch that same year, knocking him out in the 3rd round. Hamsho angered Marvin by continually butting him and Marvin decided to end the fight quickly.

Marvin Hagler knocks out Tommy Hearns in epic battle

Photograph from KO Magazine, August 1987

In April of 1985 Marvin defended against super welterweight champion Tommy Hearns. This was a meeting between two legendary champions and the fight was a classic. Both fighters fought non-stop in the first round in give and take, back and forth action. Marvin walked back to his corner with a cut over his nose.

Hearns began to tire in the 2nd round and Marvin began to take control of the fight. Hearns was exhausted by the third round of the all-out action packed bout. Marvin hurt the tiring Hearns and knocked him out with a vicious combination to the head to end the fight. Marvin proved that he had an iron chin as he took all of Hearns first round bombs without going down. It was a classic fight between two real warriors. Marvin had regained his status as a great fighter after his close fight with Roberto Duran.

Marvin was slowing down and thought about retiring after defending his title against John "The Beast" Mugabi in March of 1986. Mugabi was an Ugandan who was on a long knockout spree and was a deadly puncher. Marvin survived all of Mugabi's punches and knocked him out in the 11th round. Mugabi seemed to slow down after the 6th round but he gave Marvin a very tough fight.

Marvin was contemplating retirement until Sugar Ray Leonard announced that he wanted to come out of retirement to challenge for the middleweight title. Many of the fight experts gave Leonard little chance to win as he had been retired for several years due to eye problems. Leonard was also the naturally smaller man of the two. Leonard insisted on a twelve round fight instead of the customary fifteen rounds. Leonard had not fought in several years but the Nevada athletic commission still sanctioned the bout.

Marvin started the fight out slowly giving the first two or three rounds to Leonard. Marvin began to slowly pick the pace up but Leonard continually fought back with eye catching fast flurries to steal some of the rounds. Leonard tired somewhat towards the end of the fight but he did continue to fight back.

The fight was close and it was difficult to tell who won the fight. The judges finally awarded the fight and the title to Leonard on a split decision. The press was equally divided on who won the fight, but again many people were surprised that Leonard put up such a good fight after a lengthy absence from the ring. Marvin was unable to accept the verdict but Leonard refused to give him a rematch. Marvin eventually retired in 1988. Leonard offered him a rematch in 1990 but Marvin had moved on with his life by then, still feeling that he had really won the Leonard fight.

Marvin had a rough time adjusting to retirement and how his career had ended. He got divorced and eventually moved to Italy to start life over again. Marvin is currently married, living in Italy, and has starred in some movies there. Marvin comes back occasionally to the United States for big boxing events.

Marvin will go down in history as a deadly combination puncher. He had an iron chin and a tremendous will to win. Of his three losses, only his loss to Willie Monroe was not disputed. There is no doubt that he was the best middleweight in the world in the decade of the 1980's.

Marvin retired with a ring record of 62 wins, 3 losses, and 2 draws. He won 52 fights by knockout. He was inducted into the International Boxing Hall of Fame in 1993.

Harry Greb

Photograph from Boxing International, January 1973

Chapter Six   *No. 4 Harry Greb*

The Pittsburgh Windmill

Edward Henry "Harry" Greb was born on June 6, 1894, in Pittsburgh, Pennsylvania, to a blue collar working class family. Like Billy Papke before him, he was the son of German immigrant parents.

As a youth he was a roofer in the Pittsburgh area. He had a few amateur fights as a teenager and turned professional in 1913 as there was no money in amateur boxing. If ever a man was born to be a fighter it was Harry Greb. Managed by James Mason and George Engel, Harry fought about every week and by 1915 he was holding his own with world class fighters such as Mike and Tommy Gibbons, and George Chip. Harry was 5 feet 8 inches tall and fought at around 160 pounds.

Harry was stopped just twice in his long career. He was stopped by a much bigger Joe Chip early in his career and he suffered a broken arm in a fight with Kid Graves in 1915. Harry did not have to train much for his fights because he fought so often that his matches were used as training grounds. Harry's style of fighting was all offense. He threw punches from all angles on a non-stop basis. He had excellent footwork and, as for stamina, he could fight all night long. Harry made up for his lack of power by throwing a large volume of punches to consistently keep his opponents off balance and on the defensive.

Harry felt that part of a good defense was to have a good offense. His chin was durable and he was impossible to discourage during a fight. Some people were born to be politicians, some people were born to be lawyers but Harry Greb was born to be a fighter. With his slicked back dark hair and craggy face you did not need to ask him what his occupation was.

Harry frequently fought in flurries and he could fight at a fanatic pace for the whole fight. Harry was an all action fighter who always forced the pace and, instead of throwing one or two punch combinations, Harry would throw eight to ten punch combinations.

In 1917 Harry fought thirty-seven times and won thirty-four of the matches. Among his victims in 1917 were light heavyweights, Battling Levinsky and Jack Dillon and, former middleweight champion, George Chip. Harry also beat heavyweight "Fat" Willie Meehan, who had slapped Jack Dempsey around for a decision win. Harry beat leading middleweights and light heavyweights but he still was unable to get a world title fight in either division.

In 1918 Harry defeated Jack Dillon again and future light heavyweight champion Mike McTigue on newspaper decisions. Harry also defeated heavyweight contenders, Gunboat Smith and Billy Miske also on newspaper decisions. Harry won three newspaper decisions over top heavyweight contender Bill Brennan in 1919. Harry's ring victories read like a hall of fame list of fighters. Harry beat top contenders from middleweights on up to heavyweights and none of the champions of the three weight divisions would consider giving Harry a chance at their title. It was during a 1921 with Kid Norfolk that it was generally believed that Harry lost the sight in one eye due to being thumbed. Harry never complained as he was also guilty of thumbing opponents on multiple occasions It is no secret that Harry was considered by many to be a dirty fighter during his ring career.

Harry finally was matched with future heavyweight champion Gene Tunney for the American light heavyweight title in New York City in May of 1922. Tunney was an undefeated light heavyweight who had served in the United States Marine Corps. Tunney was a scientific fighter who was very clever and hard to beat.

Harry came roaring out of his corner in the first round and broke Tunney's nose and severely cut one of his eyes before the round was over. During the early rounds Harry cut Tunney over his other eye and Tunney fought the whole fight looking through a film of blood. Tunney received a savage beating and was barely able to finish the fight on his feet. Harry won the fifteen round decision and this was the only time Tunney ever lost a fight in his ring career.

Harry defended his light heavyweight title against challenger Tommy Loughran in New York City in January of 1923. Harry won an easy decision over Loughran as he proved to be his ring master. Loughran would go on to win the light heavyweight title and would be entered into the International Boxing Hall of fame.

Harry defended his title against Tunney in a rematch in New York City in February. Tunney had learned his lessons in the first fight and this time around he was the one who gave Harry a terrific beating over fifteen rounds to regain his title.

Harry took six months off from boxing to recover from the Tunney beating. It was rumored that he had been fighting blind in one eye since the Kid Norfolk fight in 1921. It was also falsely reported that Harry had surgery to have his eye removed and have it replaced with a glass eye.

In August of 1923, Harry was able to get Johnny Wilson to agree to defend his middleweight title against him in New York

City. Harry did not disappoint his fans as he easily won a fifteen round decision to win the world middleweight championship. Before the year was out Harry would split a pair of decisions with Loughran and lose again to Tunney in another fifteen round match.

Harry gave Wilson a rematch and defeated him again by fifteen round decision in New York City in January of 1924. Harry lost to Kid Norfolk on a foul and fought to a draw with Tommy Loughran during the year. Harry lost a newspaper decision to old foe Gene Tunney again. The problem was that Tunney was a natural light heavyweight at the time and Harry was a natural middleweight. Harry was never able to overcome Tunney's natural weight advantage after the first fight.

Harry Greb (left) defends title against Mickey Walker

Photograph from Ring Magazine, November 1973

Harry defended his title against welterweight champion Mickey Walker in July of 1925 in New York City. It was a classic match between two hall of fame fighters. It was a vicious fight with Harry coming on strong at the end of the fight to win the fifteen round decision. Legend has it that the two champions met in a nightclub after the fight and became involved in a street brawl.

By 1926 Harry was starting to lose the vision in his good eye when he defended his title against Tiger Flowers in February in New York City. Flowers was given a split decision and the title in a close fight. The verdict appeared to be fair but Harry wanted a re-match. In August Harry and Flowers fought again and Flowers won another split decision to retain his title. Harry decided to retire at this time

In October, Harry decided to have surgery on his nose to repair some damage that he had suffered in a recent automobile accident and from his years in the ring. Unfortunately Harry did not survive the surgery and he passed away at the age of 32.

Harry Greb was an incredible fighter. He fought close to 300 fights and many of them while he was blind in one eye. He beat top fighters from middleweights all the way up to heavyweights. Boxing historians have consistently rated Harry in the top five of all great middleweights and some experts believe that he is the greatest middleweight champion of all time.

Harry retired with a ring record generally accepted at 107 wins, 8 losses, and 3 draws. He won 48 fights by knockout. In 179 newspaper decision fights, Harry had 155 wins, 9 losses, and 15 draws. He was inducted into the International Boxing Hall of Fame in 1990.

Bernard Hopkins

Photograph from Ring Magazine, September 2007

Chapter Seven No. 4 Bernard Hopkins

The Executioner

Bernard Humphrey Hopkins was born on January 15, 1965, in Philadelphia, Pennsylvania. Being one of eight children and raised in poverty, it did not take long for Bernard to find trouble with the law.

By the age of 18 he had been charged with several counts of robbery. He was released from prison in 1988 after serving five years of an eighteen year sentence. When Bernard left the prison walls he vowed never to return and he never did.

Bernard did not exactly start off his professional boxing career with a bang as he lost his professional debut as a light heavyweight to an unknown fighter by the name of Clinton Mitchell. Disgusted and out of shape, Bernard took a year off from the ring before he returned to the ring in February of 1990 as a middleweight. Bernard also obtained the services of manager Bouie Fisher.

Bernard defeated Greg Page in his return to the ring and he then embarked on a twenty-two fight win streak that earned him a fight with Roy Jones for the vacant International Boxing Federation world middleweight championship in May of 1993.

Jones was undefeated and considered by many at the time to be one of the best pound for pound boxers fighting at the time. Bernard was the United States middleweight champion at the time but he was still given little chance against the talented Jones. Bernard lost by unanimous decision to Jones but it was far from an one sided fight as Bernard's counterpunching style and slick defense made the fight competitive. The judges gave Bernard four rounds in the twelve round fight and his strong showing surprised many of the boxing experts. Bernard retained his high ranking in the middleweight division and he received his second shot at the championship when Jones vacated the title in 1995.

Bernard was matched with Segundo Mercado in Quito, Ecuador, for the vacant title in December of 1994. Mercado was the hometown favorite and Bernard knew he would have to win the fight convincingly to bring the belt back to the United States. Bernard was surprisingly dropped twice early in the fight but finished strong and most of those at ringside felt that he did enough to win the decision. The judges thought otherwise and the decision was a draw. Some boxing observers felt that Bernard had not properly trained for the fight at that altitude.

The disputed decision set up a rematch which took place in Landover, Maryland, in April of 1995. This time around Bernard did not leave the decision in the judge's hands as he stopped Mercado in the 7th round to win the International Boxing Federation middleweight title.

Bernard made three title defenses in 1996. He knocked out Steve Frank in January, Joe Lipsey in March, and William Bo James in July. Improving with age Bernard swept through his competition beating, among others, Glen Johnson and John David Jackson. Bernard knocked out Simon Brown in 1998 and Robert Allen in 1999. After defeating Antwun Echols in December of 2000 a tournament was arranged with the goal of uniting the world middleweight title.

Bernard Hopkins lands a right on Bo James jaw in IBF title defense

Photograph from International Boxing Digest, September 1996

Felix Trinidad was the favorite to win the tournament as the unification series was basically designed for him to win. Trinidad knocked out William Joppy and Bernard decisioned Keith Holmes to set up the unification final in September of 2001. Trinidad was undefeated and the betting favorite in the fight. Bernard, in a huge upset, won all most every round of the fight before he finally stopped Trinidad in the final round. Bernard now held the belts to every organization and was universally recognized as the middleweight champion. This was the first time the middleweight title had been unified since Marvin Hagler retired in 1987. Bernard was named Fighter of the Year by Ring magazine and he entered the pound for pound rankings for the first time in his career.

Bernard's first mega fight was with six division champion Oscar de La Hoya in September of 2004 in Las Vegas. De la Hoya was the naturally smaller man; therefore the fight was at a catch weight of 158 pounds. Bernard had a slight lead going into the 9th round when he dropped De la Hoya with a vicious body punch. De la Hoya flopped in pain on the canvas and was counted out.

In February of 2005 Bernard decisioned Howard Eastman for his record 20th middleweight title defense. Bernard won all but one round on the judge's scorecard. Being champion for over 10 years, Bernard broke Tommy Ryan's record for holding the middleweight title for the longest time. At the age of 40 it appeared that Bernard would be champion of the division for some time to come when he was challenged by Olympian Jermaine Taylor in July of 2005. Bernard got off to his usual slow start and Taylor made the most of it by taking the early rounds. Bernard started to come on in the second half of the fight to make it close. Taylor was awarded a split decision even though it appeared Bernard did enough to retain his title in the last half of the fight.

Bernard asked for a rematch and it was held in December of 2005. In another close fight, Bernard lost by a unanimous decision to the slick boxing Taylor. With two consecutive losses in title fights it appeared that Bernard was over the hill and approaching retirement.

After taking six months off from the ring, Bernard decided to return to boxing and found new life as a light heavyweight. In Bernard's return to the ring he took on light heavyweight champion Antonio Tarver. Bernard surprised Tarver and all the boxing experts by taking a unanimous decision to win his second world title.

Bernard shut out Ronald "Winky" Wright in July of 2007 and lost a split decision to the unbeaten and future hall of fame fighter Joe Calzaghe in April of 2008. In October Bernard came back to take a surprise decision over middleweight champion Kelly Pavlik in a catch weight fight. Pavlik was a huge favorite going into the fight but Bernard made his win look easy. Bernard defeated Enrique Ornelas in December of 2009 in a return to his hometown of Philadelphia.

Bernard took on Roy Jones Jr. in a rematch seventeen years from their first fight. The fight was held in April of 2010 and Jones was definitely past his prime entering this fight. Bernard won an easy decision over Jones to gain revenge for his first title bout defeat.

In December of 2010 Bernard traveled to Quebec, Canada, to take on World Boxing Council light heavyweight champion Jean Pascal. Bernard fought a very disciplined fight but two judges ruled the fight a draw and Pascal kept his title. The World Boxing Council ordered an immediate rematch due to the controversy surrounding of the fight.

In May of 2011 Bernard returned to Canada and won an unanimous decision from Pascal in Montreal. At the age of 46 Bernard became the oldest boxing champion in history. Bernard fought Chad Dawson in a fight ruled to be a no contest in October of 2011. The fight was ruled no contest because Dawson had intentionally thrown Bernard out of the ring to end the fight. Bernard lost his title to Dawson by majority decision in a rematch in April of 2012.

In March of 2013 Bernard again surprised the boxing experts by winning a twelve round decision from unbeaten Tavoris Cloud in Brooklyn, New York, to become the International Boxing Federation light heavyweight champion. In October Bernard won an easy twelve round decision over top rated contender Karo Murat in New Jersey.

In April of 2014, ageless Bernard became the oldest fighter to ever unify a title when he dropped and took a split decision from defending World Boxing Association champion Beibut Shumenov in Washington D.C. In November, Bernard attempted to unify the light heavyweight title by taking on unbeaten Russian Sergey Kovalev. Kovalev was putting his World Boxing Organization title up against Bernard's Super World Boxing Association and International Boxing Federation titles.

Age got the best of Bernard as he was dropped in the first round and lost every single round to Kovalev. Bernard spent the year of 2015 away from boxing as he celebrated his 50th birthday. Bernard did not want to end his career on a sour note and he began looking for an opponent for one final last fight. He challenged middleweight champion Gennady Golovkin to a catch weight fight but Golovkin had other fights planned. Bernard finally settled on World Boxing Council International light heavyweight champion Joe Smith Jr. as his final opponent. Smith Jr. had won twenty-two fights and had just one loss on his record. On paper the fight appeared to be very competitive.

Bernard stepped into the ring in December of 2016 in which was to be his farewell fight. Smith Jr. started out aggressively in the first few rounds throwing bombs at Bernard. Bernard was able to defend himself and then started counter punching to make the fight close. During the 7th round, Smith Jr. trapped Bernard on the ropes and threw a six punch combination that knocked Bernard through the ropes and onto the concrete floor. Bernard appeared to have struck his head on the floor and he got up limping around. Bernard was not able to re- enter the ring and he was counted out by the referee. Smith Jr. was awarded a knockout victory and spoiled Bernard's farewell party.

It is difficult to say at this writing if the Smith Jr. fight was Bernard's last. I would say that there are no more goals for Bernard to achieve in boxing and this should have been his last fight. Bernard broke records in the middleweight division for holding the title for the longest period of time, having made the most title defenses, and being the oldest boxer to ever win a world title.

Bernard was one of the most intelligent boxers in middleweight division history. He was an excellent counterpuncher and a defensive marvel in the ring. He was an expert at pacing himself in a fight and he always appeared to be in control while in the ring. Bernard is a definite first ballot Hall of Fame fighter and his current record in boxing is 55 wins, 8 losses, and 2 draws. Bernard won 32 fights by knockout. His only knockout loss was in his last fight to Joe Smith Junior.

Stanley Ketchel

Photograph from Wikipedia

Chapter Eight   No.3 Stanley Ketchel

The Michigan Assassin

Stanislaus Kiecal was born on September 14, in 1886, to Polish immigrant parents in Grand Rapids, Michigan. As a youth he lived the life of a hobo heading west on trains. He finally stayed long enough in Butte, Montana, to work as a bouncer in a local saloon.

Stanislaus made a habit of knocking out tough miners who caused trouble in the copper mining saloons. He soon realized that he could get paid for knocking people out so he turned to professional boxing in 1903. He knocked out Kid Tracy in one round in May and had to go twenty-four rounds to knock out Mose LaFontise in August. To sound more Americanized, manager Willis Britt had Stanislaus' name changed to Stanley Ketchel. Stanley had a tremendous right hand and incredible stamina from the beginning of his career.

Stanley still needed to learn the finer points of boxing as he received boxing lessons in his two decision defeats to Maurice Thompson. Stanley knocked just about everyone else out and even had Thompson in severe trouble in their ten round draw at the end of the year. Stanley had eighteen fights all around Montana in 1905, and won them all by knockout except for a twenty round draw with Rudolph Hinz in April.

Stanley continued on his incredible knockout spree in 1906 winning six fights by knockout and fought one to a draw. Everyone out west had now heard of the incredible Polish knockout artist from Montana. He was now rated as one of the best middleweight fighters in the world. Stanley moved to California to fight world ranked opponents in 1907. Middleweight champion Tommy Ryan had just retired and the title was declared vacant. Stanley scored several more knockouts during the year and laid claim to the middleweight title when he knocked out Joe Thomas in a bloody thirty-two round battle in San Francisco, California, in September. Thomas felt that he could beat Ketchel in a rematch and it was set for December in San Francisco. Ketchel won the rematch by a convincing twenty round decision.

Mike (Twin) Sullivan had also laid claim to the middleweight title. Mike Sullivan along with his twin brother, Jack (Twin) Sullivan, were veteran battlers who had fought all of the top fighters in the welterweight and middleweight divisions. In February of 1908, Stanley knocked out Mike (Twin) Sullivan in one round to gain universal recognition as middleweight champion. In May, brother Jack (Twin) Sullivan attempted to avenge his brother's defeat. Jack did better than his brother by lasting until the twentieth round before Stanley caught up with him and knocked him cold.

In June, Stanley traveled to Milwaukee, Wisconsin, to take on unbeaten newcomer Billy Papke in a ten round non-title fight. Papke had been knocking out everybody around the Midwest and he had been asking for a title match. Stanley nearly knocked Papke out in the first round, but Papke was a rugged competitor and he survived the early beating. Papke actually came on strong in the latter half of the fight to make it competitive fight before losing a close ten round decision.

Stanley defended his title against long time contender Hugo Kelly in July in San Francisco. Stanley knocked Kelly out in three rounds and then gave a washed up Joe Thomas another chance at the title in August in San Francisco. Stanley totally dominated Thomas before mercifully knocking him out in the second round.

Billy Papke knocked out two opponents in one night in August in Boston. He knocked out Johnny Carroll in two rounds and then knocked out top contender Frank Mantell in one round in the second half of his double header. As a result, Ketchel finally relented to give Papke a title fight in September in Los Angeles, California.

In one of the most controversial fights in history, Stanley was knocked down five times in the first round by Papke. Some newspapers reported that Papke hit Ketchel when he went to shake hands before the fight. Other newspapers made no mention of this pre-fight activity on Papke's part. Ketchel was a bloody mess when he went back to his corner at the end of the first round. Stanley's nose was broken, he had one eye closed, and he had a serious cut over one of his eyes. In modern times a corner man or referee would have stopped this fight but in 1908 Ketchel was expected to carry on. Ketchel came out for the 2nd round, but he had no chance of winning as he was already a beaten man. Ketchel tried to fight back but he had no power in his punches and he took a terrific beating. He was dropped in the 11th round, and finally in the 12th round he was unable to beat the ten count after taking a particularly hard punch. After the fight, Ketchel laid on the table with one eye closed, the other cut, nose broken, and lumps all over his head. Through split lips, Ketchel vowed vengeance on Papke and said that he should have been ready to fight at the beginning. Stanley did not blame a foul at the start of the fight for his defeat. One of his corner men, Pete Stone, told the press that his fighter had been fouled at the start of the fight.

The rematch took place in late November, on Thanksgiving Day in 1908, in Los Angeles. Stanley was at his most vicious best in this fight. There was no handshake at the start of this fight and Stanley came out swinging. Stanley beat Papke to the punch in every round and he seemed to be enjoying the systematic beating he was giving Papke. Ketchel finally decided to end the slaughter in the 11th and dropped Papke near the ropes for the ten count. Papke would claim that he could not hear the ten count due to the crowd noise, but he appeared to be a thoroughly beaten man at the time.

Stanley Ketchel (right) regains Middleweight title from Billy Pakpe

Photograph from Boxing International All Star Wrestling, July 1965

Stanley became the first man to ever regain the middleweight championship. Not one to rest on his laurels, Stanley took on former light heavyweight champion, Philadelphia Jack O'Brien, in March of 1909, in New York City. The fight ended with O'Brien knocked out cold. The bell saved O'Brien at the end of the fight and the match was declared a No Decision. In June Stanley fought a rematch with O'Brien and knocked him out easily in the 3rd round.

Stanley had a goal of winning the heavyweight championship. Before Stanley could challenge for the heavyweight title he had to first dispose of former rival Billy Papke. Papke had been telling the press that Stanley was ducking him and afraid to give him a rematch to finally prove who was the better fighter. Stanley never backed away from a challenge and in July of 1909 he took on Papke for the fourth time in the San Francisco suburb of Colma, California. The fighters agreed to a twenty round fight with the middleweight title on the line.

There was no handshake again at the start of this fight. The two fighters battled toe to toe for the whole twenty rounds. They were both blood smeared and neither fighter took a backward step during the whole fight. The fight was close and competitive but Ketchel had a slight edge in the fight. Referee Billy Roche walked over to Ketchel's corner after the end of the fight and raised his hand as to the winner of the fight. The verdict was generally accepted by the spectators and the press. Papke would only state that he felt that he should have received at least a draw in the fight.

In October of 1909, Stanley challenged heavyweight champion Jack Johnson for the title. Rumors floated about that Ketchel and Johnson agreed to battle to a draw to set up a lucrative rematch with both fighters trying their best to win the second fight. Ketchel came out fast and did not appear to be a man fighting an exhibition match as he was swinging wildly with power punches. Johnson defended well and kept Stanley off of him with a long jab. By the twelfth round, Stanley's face was a bloody mess.

Finally in the twelfth round Stanley connected with a wild right hand punch that lands behinds Johnsons ear, sending him to the canvas. The crowd went wild. Johnson took an eight count and then got up. Stanley rushed in wildly to finish the fight when he ran straight into a Johnson punch which knocked him out cold. It would be written that Johnson found Stanley's front teeth imbedded into his glove.

Stanley took five months off from boxing after the Johnson defeat. Finally in March of 1910, Stanley started to get back into the ring to get in shape by boxing exhibitions with top middleweights Frank Klaus and Sam Langford. Both Langford and Klaus matches were no decision fights. In May, Stanley knocked out Porky Flynn and Willie Lewis. In June, Stanley knocked out Jim Smith in New York City in five rounds.

Stanley took the summer off from boxing and in October he accepted an invitation from a personal friend named Colonel R.P. Dickerson to come and stay at his ranch in Conway, Missouri. Ketchel, who was known as a womanizer, apparently made advances towards a cook named Goldie Smith at the ranch. Smith's boyfriend, Walter Dipley, also worked at the ranch and became angry at Ketchel's arrogant attitude and advances towards his girlfriend. Dipley was afraid to confront Ketchel but one morning, when Stanley was having breakfast, Dipley shot him in the back with his .22 caliber rifle. Ketchel died hours later at a hospital at the age of 24 from the gunshot wound.

Due to the circumstances of his death, and at a young age, Ketchel became something of a cult figure to the boxing world. Fellow boxers made pilgrimages to Ketchel's gravesite in Michigan and, due to his bohemian lifestyle, the press loved to write about him. Ketchel's lifestyle coupled with his dynamite right hand punch in the ring made him a legend to the adoring boxing public. Ketchel was largely considered the greatest middleweight champion during the first half of the 20th century until the appearance of Sugar Ray Robinson in the 1950's.

Stanley Ketchel was truly a legendary champion. His knockout power was rivaled only by Bob Fitzsimmons in the middleweight division and, with his incredible stamina, he could knock you out early or late into a fight.

Stanley's final ring record was 51 wins, with 4 losses and 4 draws. He won 48 fights by knockout. His record in newspaper decisions was 2 wins, 1 loss, 1 draw, and 1 no contest. He was inducted into the International Boxing Hall of Fame in 1990.

Sugar Ray Robinson

Photograph from Boxing 89, September 1989

Chapter Nine   *No. 2 Sugar Ray Robinson*

Pound for Pound

Sugar Ray Robinson has been called by many experts as the greatest pound for pound fighter ever. Many boxing publications including Ring Magazine have named him the greatest middleweight champion ever.

Sugar Ray Robinson was born Walker Smith on May 3, 1921, in Ailey, Georgia. While boxing as an amateur as Walker Smith he won the Golden Gloves featherweight title in 1939 and the Golden Gloves lightweight title in New York in 1940. He was undefeated as an amateur.

Walker Smith assumed the ring name of Sugar Ray Robinson when he turned professional. Ray turned professional under the management of George Gainford, in October of 1940, with a two round knockout of Joe Echevarria.

By 1941, Ray was defeating world class fighters such as National Boxing Association future lightweight champion Sammy Angott, future welterweight champion Marty Servo, and former welterweight champion Fritzie Zivic.

In 1942, Ray defeated Zivic and Servo in rematches, and also decisioned future middleweight champion, Jake LaMotta. Sammy Angott had won the world lightweight title after his first match with Ray in 1941. Ray decisioned Angott again in the over the lightweight limit rematch. In February of 1943 Ray stepped into a Detroit ring to face LaMotta in a rematch with a perfect record of forty wins and no losses. Ray was dropped and lost a ten round decision to LaMotta to suffer his first defeat as a professional. Three weeks later, in the same Detroit ring, Ray won the rubber match with LaMotta by taking an easy ten round decision.

Ray finished out 1943 by beating his idol, former three time world champion Henry Armstrong by a decision. It appeared that at any time in the fight Ray could have stopped Armstrong but chose to let him finish the fight due to the respect that he had for the former champion.

Ray won five bouts in 1944 before he was inducted into the United States army. Ray continued fighting while in the army and he defeated his old nemesis Jake LaMotta twice, by decision, in 1945. Ray was the number one contender for the welterweight title when he got out of the army but it was Marty Servo who got the title shot against champion Freddie "Red" Cochrane in February of 1946. Servo knocked Cochrane out in four rounds to take the title and was ordered by the boxing commissions to defend against Ray. Servo instead took on middleweight Rocky Graziano in an over the weight match. Graziano broke Servo's nose and knocked him out in two rounds. Servo chose to retire due to his nose injury instead of facing Ray.

Ray took on tough Artie Levine while waiting for a shot at the welterweight title in Cleveland in November. Levine was a hard puncher and he dropped Ray hard in the 5th round of their fight with a left hook. Ray barely beat the count before the bell rang ending the round. It took Ray a few rounds to clear his head and then he came out fast in the 10th round and swarmed all over Levine before stopping him in the final round.

The National Boxing Association set up a bout between Ray and veteran welterweight Tommy Bell to fight for the welterweight title. The fight for the vacated title was set for December of 1946 in New York City. Ray had defeated Bell by decision in 1945 and took him lightly as an opponent.

Ray started off slow and was dropped by a Bell left hook in the 7th round. Ray landed face first when he hit the canvas but got up and survived the round. After ten rounds the fight was still close. In the 11th round Ray dropped Bell and swept the remaining rounds to win a unanimous decision and the welterweight title. Ray had, at last, reached his goal of a world championship but he also had his sights on the middleweight championship as well.

In June of 1947, Ray defended his title against a tough journeyman named Jimmy Doyle. The fight took place in Cleveland, Ohio. Doyle was an aggressive type of fighter who had been fighting out of Los Angeles. Doyle had recently defeated Ralph Zanelli and Danny Kapilow to earn the title fight.

Doyle held his own with Ray for the first seven rounds. In the 8th round Ray beat Doyle to the punch with a left hook which dropped him hard to the canvas. Doyle hit the canvas with his seat first, then his shoulders, and then his head in a whip like motion. Doyle attempted to stir at the count of four but fell back down to the canvas. At the count of nine the bell rang but Jimmy Doyle never did get up and he died the day after the fight.

Ray fought a few exhibition matches and gave the proceeds of the matches to Jimmy Doyle's widow. After the exhibition matches, Ray returned to the ring in August of 1947. He won a few tune up fights before defending his title against Chuck Taylor in December in Detroit. Ray never looked better and he stopped Taylor in six rounds.

In June of 1948, Ray defended his title against New Orleans based welterweight Bernard Docusen in Chicago. Docusen was a legitimate top contender and Ray won a convincing fifteen round decision over the crafty fighter. In September Ray took on the flashy Cuban Kid Gavilan. Gavilan was known for his bolo punching and aggressive style of fighting. Ray took the ten round decision but the Cuban Kid turned out to be a tougher opponent than expected.

Ray fought as a middleweight during the first half of 1949 but Kid Gavilan was hollering for a title fight based upon his strong showing against Ray in the 1948. Ray granted Gavilan his wish and defended his title against him in Philadelphia in July. As expected Gavilan again proved to be a tough opponent, but Ray won a unanimous decision to prove to the Cuban that he was still the boss in the welterweight division. Gavilan had his moments in the fight but Ray turned out to be the better all-around fighter, taking nine of the fifteen rounds on the judge's scorecards.

Ray was finding it difficult to make the welterweight limit of 147 pounds and he began taking on middleweights on a regular basis. In June of 1950 he won Pennsylvania recognition as middleweight champion by taking an easy fifteen round decision over Robert Villemain in Philadelphia. In August Ray made the last defense of his welterweight title when he won a fifteen round decision over an overmatched Charley Fusari in Jersey City. Two weeks after the Fusari fight, Ray defended his Pennsylvania middleweight title by knocking out Jose Basora in one round.

In October Ray knocked out Carl "Bobo" Olson in the 12th round in his defense of his middleweight title. He then set his sights on fighting world middleweight champion Jake LaMotta. Ray had beat LaMotta several times before but LaMotta had also handed Ray his only defeat going into their title fight. The title match was finally set for St. Valentine 's Day in February of 1951, in Chicago.

The fight which would later be referred to as "The St. Valentine's Day Massacre" began slowly with LaMotta picking up the pace around the 3rd round. LaMotta fought his usual aggressive fight, trying to get in close and work Ray's body. Ray took LaMotta's best punches then took over the fight around the 10th round as LaMotta appeared to tire. Ray was battering a defenseless LaMotta against the ropes in the 13th round when the referee mercifully stepped in to save LaMotta from further punishment. Sugar Ray won the middleweight title after fighting professionally for eleven years.

Sugar Ray Robinson wins the title from Jake LaMotta

Photograph from Boxing Scene, April 1985

Ray gave up the welterweight title and went on a European tour with his huge boxing entourage. Ray made stops in France, Germany, and Italy taking on local opponents before finally defending his title against Randy Turpin in July of 1951, in London.

Ray was not in top shape and totally underestimated Turpin's skills. Turpin was a strong middleweight who the British press wrote had "a ruffian style of boxing". Turpin jumped all over Ray from the beginning of the fight and Ray could not keep Turpin off of him. In the 7th round Ray suffered a cut eye from what he would later claim was a head butt. Turpin outpunched Ray throughout the whole fight and Ray knew that he had lost at the end of the 15th round. The referee had the only vote and he voted for Turpin. The decision was just and Turpin was the new champion. Ray returned to the United States as an ex-champion but he had a return match clause in his contract for the Turpin fight. Ray exercised his right to the return match and it was to take place in September in New York City.

Ray was in top shape and totally prepared for the rematch. After nine rounds Ray was slightly ahead in the fight when, in the 10th round, his old cut from the first fight opened up after a Turpin butt. Ray realized that the cut was bad and that the referee might stop the fight. Ray attacked Turpin and dropped him with a left to the midsection and a right hand smash to the jaw. Turpin was up at the count of seven but his left eye was half closed. Ray attacked Turpin again and drove him across the ring, throwing thirty-one punches in 25 seconds. Turpin was in a bent over position when the referee stopped the fight and awarded it to Ray. Ray had come back from the brink of defeat to regain his title.

In March of 1952, Ray defended his title against old foe Carl "Bobo" Olson. Olson put up a surprisingly good fight against Ray who had to come on strong in the last few rounds to gain the decision. Ray defended against former middleweight champion Rocky Graziano in Chicago. Graziano was past his prime but still managed to drop Ray for a flash knockdown before getting knocked out in the 3rd round.

After cleaning out the middleweight division of contenders, Ray set his sights on champion Joey Maxim's light heavyweight title. Joey Maxim was a classy slick boxing light heavyweight from Cleveland Ohio. Maxim had won the title from Freddie Mills in London in 1950 and had successfully defended his title against Irish Bob Murphy in 1951. The fight was set for June of 1952 in New York City. Maxim had about a seventeen pound weight advantage going into the fight and, at 6 foot 1 inch, he was two inches taller than Ray. New York City was in the middle of an unusual heat wave and it was well over 100 degrees inside of the ring.

Ray started out the fight hooking and jabbing and dancing circles around Maxim. It was obvious in the early rounds that Ray was much faster than Maxim but it was also apparent that Maxim, due to his size advantage, was able to take Ray's best punches and keep coming forward. At the end of ten rounds Ray was comfortably ahead in the fight on points but the referee had to be replaced due to the intense heat. A new referee was brought in as a replacement and the fight continued. It became apparent that after the 10th round Ray was slowing down but still leading on points.

By the 13th round, Ray was stumbling around the ring due to the intense heat and fell flat on his face after missing a wild punch. Maxim began to attack Ray as the bell rang to end the round. Ray was totally exhausted and suffering from heat prostration. Ray was unable to come out of his corner for the 14th round and Maxim was awarded a 14th round technical knockout win. At the end of the fight, the scorecards showed that Ray was ahead ten rounds to three and he just needed to finish the fight on his feet to win the decision.

After recovering from the fight Ray decided that he wished to retire from the ring to go into show business. Ray traveled around the country and Europe and did a song and dance routine. Ray achieved moderate success but, by the end of 1954, he wished to fight again.

Ray began his comeback on January 5, 1955, by knocking out veteran trial horse Joe Rindone in six rounds. Two weeks later, on January 19th, Ray signed to meet veteran Ralph "Tiger" Jones in Chicago. Jones was a favorite of the television networks as he was an aggressive battler who was never in a boring fight.

It was obvious from the beginning that Ray had not got into total fighting shape as Jones bulled him around the ring and won nine out of the ten rounds on the judge's scorecards. The writers were cruel to Ray as they were writing about his ring obituary and how he should retire. Ray decided not to retire and he won several fights by knockout to set up a title eliminator fight with number one contender Rocky Castellani. Castellani had lost a decision to the new champion Carl "Bobo" Olson in 1954 in a title match and he was trying to get back into the title picture. Ray was a 3 to 1 underdog to Castellani in the betting for the fight. The fight was set up for July of 1955 in San Francisco.

Ray started off well in the fight, working the midsection, until everything changed in the 6th round. Castellani caught Ray with a right to the head, a left hook, and a clubbing right to the head that dropped Ray to the canvas. Ray was hurt but still managed to get up at the count of nine. Ray used an old trick by putting one hand on the top rope and sliding back and forth in the ring to confuse Castellani. This trick bought Ray enough time to clear his head and finish the round. Ray coasted in round seven and then swept the last three rounds to win a split decision and a shot at Olson's title.

Olson had failed in an attempt to take Archie Moore's light heavyweight title in June and his defense against Ray was set for December of 1955 in Chicago. Ray was again a huge underdog as

Olson, after winning the vacated title in 1953, had made successful title defenses against Kid Gavilan, Castellani, and Pierre Langlois in 1954.

The veteran trainer, Jack Blackburn, had developed Ray into an aggressive finisher when he had a man hurt in the ring. In the second round of his title fight, with Olson wobbling in front of him, he ripped a right uppercut and left hook to drop Olson flat on his back. Olson rolled over in an attempt to beat the count but he did not make it. Ray was the middleweight champion for the third time.

Ray gave Olson a rematch in May of 1956 in Los Angeles and he knocked him out this time in the 4th round. Ray had won all four fights that he had with Olson, with three of them by knockout. In January of 1957, Ray defended against bull like Gene Fullmer from Utah. The match was held in New York City. Fullmer was a rough, crude type of brawler who always seemed to do everything wrong in the ring but still found a way to win. Fullmer was also accused of being a dirty fighter as he frequently led with his head when attacking an opponent.

Ray was unable to solve Fullmer's awkward aggressive style in the ring and at the end of fifteen rounds Ray was declared the loser and an ex-champion again. Without taking any tune ups fights Ray challenged Fullmer again for the title in a rematch in Chicago.

Ray was doing better in the rematch but Fullmer was still ahead in the fight with his bull like rushes. In the 5th round, Ray timed one of Fullmer's rushes and hit him with a picture perfect left hook to the chin. Fullmer dropped immediately and was unable to get up before the ten count. Ray was a champion for the 4th time, and this was the first time that Fullmer had ever been knocked out.

In September of 1957, Ray gave welterweight champion Carmen Basilio a shot at his title. Basilio was a tough little onion farmer from Canastota, New York. He was a two time welterweight champion and he had cleaned his division out of welterweight contenders. The fight was held in New York City and the fight turned out to be a war.

Basilio was the aggressor throughout the fight but Ray counterpunched well to keep the fight even. The spectators were surprised what a terrific showing Basilio made in the fight. It appeared to be a case of a good little man beating a good big man in the ring. At the end of fifteen rounds of non-stop action Basilio was awarded the title on a split decision. It was a very gutsy performance on Basilio's behalf and the boxing public wanted to see a rematch. The rematch took place in March of 1958 in Chicago.

Early in the rematch, Basilio received a cut over one of his eyes and he fought most of the battle with one eye closed and horribly swollen. Basilio still remained competitive in the fight but this time Ray was able to control the smaller man and take a fifteen round split decision. Ray had just won the middleweight title for the 5th time but due to all the ring wars he was slowing down.

Negotiations for a rubber match with Basilio stalled over the issue of money and Ray did not defend his title at all in 1959. Because of this lack of defenses Ray was stripped of his title by the National Boxing Association in 1959. Ray was still recognized as world champion in New York and Massachusetts.

In January of 1960, Ray defended his share of the title against local fighter Paul Pender in Boston. Pender was a good boxer but was not much of a knockout threat. Pender had a history of brittle hands and had been inactive for long periods of time. In a boring fight, Ray lost a split decision and what was left of his middleweight title. It appeared that Ray had definitely lost a step in the ring. In June Ray returned to Boston and ended up with the same result as he lost another fifteen round split decision to Pender.

In December Ray challenged Gene Fullmer for the National Boxing Association middleweight title in Los Angeles. Ray put on one of his best performances in years and many boxing experts felt that he deserved the decision. The judges ruled the fight a draw and Fullmer kept his title.

Fullmer gave Ray a rematch in March of 1961 in Las Vegas. This time around there was no question about the decision as Fullmer took a clear cut unanimous decision. This was to be the last time Ray fought for the middleweight championship.

This was probably the time that Ray should have retired but, like most older fighters, it was hard for him to give up the sport. Ray fought on all the way up to 1965 beating some contenders and losing to others. Ray lost to fighters he would have beat easily in his prime. Ray finally retired after light punching Joey Archer dropped him and took a unanimous decision in Pittsburgh in November of 1965.

"Flashy", could best describe Sugar Ray Robinson. Ray had a ton of natural talent and a natural rhythm in the ring. He was deadly with his rapid fire double left hooks and he exhibited a sense of balance and power in the ring. Ray could also be described as "a natural" in the ring. Many boxing experts feel that he may have been, pound for pound, the greatest fighter in history and also the greatest middleweight champion who ever entered the ring. If Stanley Ketchel was thought to be the greatest middleweight champion of the first half of the 20th century, then Ray was thought to be the greatest middleweight champion during the second half of the century.

Ray retired with a ring record of 173 wins, 19 losses, 6 draws, and 2 no contests. Ray won 108 fights by knockout. He passed away in 1989 at the age of 67 and was inducted into the International Boxing Hall of Fame in 1990.

Carlos Monzon

Photograph from Murderpedia.com

Chapter Ten   No. 1 Carlos Monzon

Monzon the Magnificent

Carlos Roque Monzon was born in Santa Fe, Argentina, on August 7. 1942. One of twelve children Carlos grew up in the slums of Santa Fe shining shoes and selling newspapers in the streets. As a youth he also spent time in jail for fighting in the streets and starting a brawl at a sporting event.

Carlos spent most of his youth in jail and he is lucky that well known Argentine manager, Amilcar Brusa, also coached the police boxing team. Brusa saw the intense fire and hunger in the eyes of the youthful Monzon and turned him professional at the age of 20 in 1963. Starting out as a pure slugger, he knocked out his first eight opponents before he lost a ten round decision to tough Argentine middleweight, Antonio Aguilar.

Brusa did not protect his fighter to build up an unbeaten record on soft opponents. Carlos won four more fights by knockout and developed a very cocky attitude in the ring. In June of 1964, Brusa took Carlos to Rio de Janeiro, Brazil, to take on tough veteran middleweight Felipe Cambeiro. The difference in experience was evident as Cambeiro was able to survive Carlos' bombs in the ring and walk away with a deserving decision. Brusa had put Carlos in the ring with Cambeiro to show him that he still had a lot to learn at this stage of his career.

Carlos returned to the ring to record five more victories before he suffered the final defeat of his career when he dropped a ten round decision to Alberto Massi. Brusa advised Carlos that he had to give up his street fighting days and train properly in the gym if he wanted a career in boxing. At this point Carlos vowed to never lose another fight.

In 1965, Carlos defeated the Argentine veteran Andres Selpa and traveled to Sao Paulo, Brazil, in August to defeat Felipe Cambeiro in a rematch. In October, Carlos also defeated Antonio Aguilar by decision in another rematch.

In September of 1966, Carlos defeated world ranked middleweight Jorge Fernandez with a twelve round decision to win the Argentine middleweight championship. In December, Carlos defended his title by knocking out Alberto Massi in a rematch. Carlos had now reversed all three of his previous losses.

In February of 1967, Carlos defeated Alberto Massi again and, in May, took on tough middleweight veteran Bennie Briscoe. In a rough and grueling fight, Carlos was lucky to walk away with a draw with the tough Philadelphia fighter. In June Carlos again defeated Jorge Fernandez for the South American middleweight championship. After winning the South American title Carlos found himself in the world top ten middleweight rankings.

In 1968, Carlos defeated Alberto Massi and beat Juan Aguilar twice. In January of 1969, Carlos knocked out Ruben Orrico in a South American middleweight title defense and in August he won a ten round decision from world ranked Tom Bethea in Buenos Aires. In September Carlos made another South American middleweight title defense by knocking out Manuel Severino in eight rounds.

In February of 1970, Carlos again beat Antonio Aguilar and in August won a ten round decision from American Eddie Pace.

Carlos had now quietly worked his way up to the number one middleweight contender position for Nino Benvenuti's middleweight title.

Argentine promoter Tito Lectoure, along with Italian promoter Rodolfo Sabatini, arranged the title match for Carlos. The fight with Benvenuti was to be held in Rome in November. Benvenuti was a huge favorite as Carlos had done almost all of his fighting in Argentina and was unknown in the United States and Europe. Benvenuti was a popular champion and he did not appear to see Carlos as a threat to his title. Benvenuti angered Carlos at the weigh in as Carlos felt that Benvenuti was making fun of his masculinity.

Carlos took control of the fight from the beginning and surprised Benvenuti with his power. It was obvious in the ring that Carlos was the stronger fighter as he was throwing Benvenuti around in the clinches and clubbing him at will with his power punches. Benvenuti tried to fight back and did well in spurts, but Carlos continued to control the fight. At the end of eleven rounds, ringside officials had only given three rounds to Benvenuti. Benvenuti looked tired as he came out for the 12th round. Carlos drove Nino across the ring with a flurry and dropped him with a hard right hand to the jaw. Nino laid on the canvas in a shell like position before he got up just before the ten count. The referee took one look at Benvenuti as he staggered back into the ropes and stopped the fight. The fans in the audience were in shock at what they had just observed. Their hero Nino Benvenuti had just been knocked out by this unknown South American fighter. The only people who were not surprised by the outcome in the whole arena were Carlos and his manager, Amilcar Brusa.

Carlos returned to Argentina as the middleweight champion of the world. Most people in Argentina were also surprised that he had won the title. Most of his previous opponents in South America were not considered to be in the same class as Benvenuti.

Carlos scored knockouts in Argentina in a couple of tune up fights and then signed to defend his title against Benvenuti in a rematch in May of 1971, in Monte Carlo. Some ring observers thought that Benvenuti just had an off night and that he would rebound in the rematch to regain his title. Carlos proved the experts wrong again as he made quick work of Benvenuti. Carlos knocked Benvenuti down and threw him around in the clinches again. Benvenuti's corner saw that he had no hope of winning and they threw the towel in the ring in the 3rd round to save their fighter from further punishment. Carlos erased any doubts that he was the best middleweight in the world. In September, former three time welterweight and two time middleweight champion Emile Griffith traveled to Buenos Aires to challenge Carlos in September of 1971.

Griffith put up a struggle for ten rounds before Carlos began to control the fight with his superior power. Carlos finally stopped the game old warrior in the 14th round. Carlos had a banner year in 1972, defending his title on four occasions. In March of 1972, he stopped Denny Moyer in five rounds in Rome. Carlos was winning the fight but it appeared that the Italian referee did stop the fight too soon.

In June, Carlos traveled to Paris to defend his title against no. 1 contender Jean Claude Bouttier. Bouttier was a good boxer but he found Carlos too powerful and he was finally stopped in the 12th round. In August, Carlos went to Copenhagen, Denmark, to take on local Tom Bogs. Bogs cut Carlos in the fight and the cut seemed to spur Carlos on as he stopped Bogs in the 5th round.

In Buenos Aires, in November, Carlos fought a rematch with, always tough contender, Bennie Briscoe. Carlos was lucky to get a draw in their first fight and this time the title was on the line. Carlos was well ahead in the fight when Briscoe hit him with a left hook in the 9th round that made Carlos grab the ropes. Briscoe for some reason did not follow up his advantage and Carlos escaped the knockout. Carlos continued to pile up points in the fight and he was awarded a fair, unanimous decision over the Philadelphia battler. Based on his four successful title defenses, Carlos was named Fighter of the Year by various boxing publications for the year 1972.

Carlos defended his title twice in 1973 by winning unanimous decisions over Jean Claude Bouttier and Emile Griffith in rematches. Boxing experts cited the fact that he had previously knocked out both Bouttier and Griffith so they felt that Carlos was slipping. The truth was that Carlos was having domestic problems at home. During the year Carlos wife, Beatriz Garcia, shot him twice during a domestic quarrel.

Welterweight champion Jose Napoles was the next challenger for Carlos' title. Many boxing experts felt that Napoles had a chance against Carlos because the middleweight champion did not look sharp in his title defenses in 1973 and Napoles was a sharp counterpuncher who had wiped out all of his welterweight competition in his last three successful title defenses.

Monzon defended against Napoles in February of 1974. Carlos was simply too big, too strong, and too young for Napoles to beat. Carlos dismantled Napoles in a methodical way that had him cut and totally beat at the end of seven rounds. Napoles did not come out for the 8th round as he had no fight left in him. The world now knew just how great Carlos Monzon was. Monzon's style was described by the press as coolly efficient. After this fight for some unknown reason the World Boxing Council decided to strip Carlos of their recognition as middleweight champion. The World Boxing Association and everyone else still considered him to be the champion.

Weak chinned Tony Mundine traveled to Buenos Aires to be stopped in seven rounds by Carlos in his last title defense of the year. In June, Monzon made his only United States appearance when he defended against Tony Licata in New York City. Licata was a boxer, not a puncher, and he spent most of the early rounds circling away from Carlos. Carlos finally caught up to him in the 10th round when he dropped him and the referee stopped the fight. Apparently the United States press was not impressed with Carlos' style as a Sports Illustrated writer compared his style to being "as stiff as a cigar store Indian".

Carlos traveled to Paris, which was becoming his favorite place to fight. Carlos defended against Frenchman Gratien Tonna. Tonna was a hard puncher but he had been known to quit when the going got rough. True to form, Tonna refused to get up from a punch he claimed hit him in the back of the head in the 5th round. The referee counted Tonna out and Carlos was given the knockout win.

Carlos was still married but was spending all of his time running around Europe with Argentine actress, Susanna Giminez. Carlos wished to retire and go into making movies but he still wanted to unify the title before he retired. In June of 1976 a title unification match was set up between him and World Boxing Council champion Rodrigo Valdes in Monte Carlo. Valdes, a Colombian, had won the vacant title in 1974 and had made four successful defenses of his title. Valdez was thought to be a dangerous opponent for Carlos.

Shortly before the fight, Rodrigo's brother had been murdered in Colombia but he still chose to go on with the fight. Carlos started off strong and took most of the early rounds. Valdes made a comeback during the middle rounds, and was doing well until Carlos knocked him down through the ropes in the 14th round. Carlos took the last two rounds and won a close unanimous decision.

Valdes asked for a rematch by claiming that his brother's death just before the fight affected his performance. The closeness of the first fight was another reason given for a rematch. Carlos agreed to the rematch and it was set for July of 1977 in Monte Carlo again.

Carlos Monzon lands a solid right to Rodrigo Valdes' head

Photograph from The Ring, November 1977

This time around it was Valdes who started off fast by dropping Carlos for a flash knockdown in the second round with an overhand right. During the middle rounds Carlos adjusted to Valdes aggressive style and began to sidestep him and hit him with right hands. Valdes was severely cut by one of the right hands and Carlos finished strong winning a clear cut unanimous decision. Carlos proved he was still the best middleweight in the world but at the age of 35 he decided to retire and make movies with his girlfriend, Susanna Giminez.

By this time Carlos was divorced from his first wife but domestic issues seemed to plague him as Giminez was seen walking around Argentina wearing dark glasses to cover her blackened eyes. Carlos had never been able to control his temper outside of the ring and it would eventually prove to be his undoing.

Carlos continued making movies but he separated from Giminez around 1979. Rumor had it that Carlos spent most of his free time playing cards and going to night clubs.

Around the end of 1979 he met Alicia Muniz and got married. Carlos had one son with Muniz but his relationship with her was also tumultuous. Carlos and Muniz separated but got together on Valentine's Day in 1988 in Mar de Plata. Carlos and Muniz argued and during the argument both of them fell over a balcony. Carlos injured his arm and Muniz died from her injuries. Carlos was arrested for murder and the jury found him guilty when it was proved that Muniz had been choked unconscious before she fell from the balcony.

Carlos was given an eleven year prison sentence in 1989 and died while returning to the prison from a weekend pass in 1995 in a one car automobile accident. Despite his domestic difficulties, Carlos is still revered as a hero in Argentina by the sporting public. He always appeared to be in control in the ring. He had a solid chin, was rarely cut, had a terrific left jab, and had a strong right hand. His face was also unmarked as he was seldom hit with a solid punch. His final ring record was 87 wins, 3 losses, 9 draws, and 1 no contest. He won 59 fights by knockout. He reversed all three of his early losses in rematches. Carlos was inducted into the International Boxing Hall of Fame in 1990.

Chapter Eleven   *Analysis of Rankings*

RATING THE CHAMPIONS:

My boxing chart for rating my selection of my 10 greatest middleweight champions consists of the following categories and descriptions:

Boxing Skill: The ability to punch accurately and slip or block an opponent's punches. Fast hands, combination punching, and good footwork contribute to high marks in this category

Power Punching: The ability to knock out opponents with one solid blow or in a series of powerful punches delivered with deadly accuracy

Dominance of Division: The ability to win the championship and to successfully defend the title against all of the top contenders in a convincing manner for a lengthy period of time, such as a decade.

Quality of opposition: To be able to defeat all of the available top contenders in the division who pose a serious threat to the title over the period of the champion's reign.

Stamina: The ability to finish a fight strong and to maintain a high work rate during the fight. The ability to go the whole distance at top speed all night long.

Defense: The ability to slip and block an opponent's punches. Aggressive boxers with excellent bob and weave styles also do well in this category.

OFFICIAL CHAMPIONS CHARTS

	BOXING SKILL	POWER	DOMINANCE OF DIVISION	QUALITY OF OPPOSITION	STAMINA	DEFENSE	DETER-MINATION	CONSIS-TENCY	PRONE TO CUTS	DURABILITY	TOTAL
CARLOS MONZON	9	9	10	10	10	10	10	10	10	10	98
SUGAR RAY ROBINSON	10	10	10	10	10	9	10	9	9	10	97
STANLEY KETCHEL	8	10	10	10	10	9	10	10	9	10	96
HARRY GREB	10	8	9	10	10	9	10	10	9	10	95
BERNARD HOPKINS	10	9	10	10	9	10	9	9	9	10	95
MARVIN HAGLER	9	9	10	10	9	9	9	10	9	10	94
BOB FITZSIMMONS	8	10	9	10	10	8	10	10	8	10	93
MARCEL CERDAN	9	9	9	10	9	10	9	9	9	9	92
TONY ZALE	8	9	10	10	10	8	10	8	8	10	91
NINO BENVENUTI	10	8	9	9	9	9	9	9	9	9	90

Determination: The will to win when facing defeat and adversity in the ring. The attitude of never giving up in a fight until the final bell.

Consistency: To win and successfully defend the title during the champions peak years. Boxers who retire as champions after defending the title over an extended period of time score better then boxers who become champions then lose and regain the title several times.

Prone to cuts: To be able to complete a fight without being stopped due to cuts. To be able to fight without cuts affecting the outcome of the fight.

Durability: To be able to sustain a significant amount of punishment, and come back strong to win a fight. To be able to outlast an opponent to gain the victory.

ANALYSIS THAT DETERMINED THE RANKINGS:

Carlos Monzon, in my opinion was the greatest of all the middleweight champions. Was he greater then Sugar Ray Robinson, Stanley Ketchell, Harry Greb, and Bernard Hopkins? The answer is yes he was. He dominated his era of boxing like no other middleweight champion, including Sugar Ray Robinson. He participated in a total of fifteen world championship fights. He won all fifteen. He won ten by knockout and five by unanimous decision. He was rarely cut and, maybe, knocked down only once or twice in his career. He fought, and beat, all the top contenders of his era and he avenged all three of his early defeats. He was undefeated for the last thirteen years of his career. Carlos had a stiff left jab, followed by a quick hard right cross. His left hook was underestimated and he was so physically strong that he would simply manhandle his opponents. His defense was superb. He leaned away from punches just at the right time and his height (6 foot) made it easy for him to lean out of an opponent's punching range. He had perfect timing in the ring and had pinpoint accuracy. He rarely wasted his punches. He faced a talented welterweight champion in Jose Napoles, and he proved to be too big and strong for him, slicing him up in seven rounds.

He methodically, but unspectacularly, wore opponents down. Would he have beaten Robinson in a head to head fight? I believe the Monzon of 1972 would have defeated the Ray Robinson of 1952. I think the fight would have been a replay of the first Turpin vs. Robinson fight of 1951 which Turpin won by decision. I believe Robinson would have started off fast, won some early rounds, and may have stunned Monzon once or twice. In the end I believe Carlos would have worn Ray down to take a unanimous decision. He also knew when to retire. He retired on top and never returned to the ring.

Sugar Ray Robinson has been called the best fighter, pound for pound, but in my opinion he was the second best middleweight champion of all time. Ray probably had the most natural talent of all the middleweight champions and he may have been the best welterweight champion of all time. As welterweight champion from 1946 to 1951 he was totally unbeatable.

Ray was a five time middleweight champion. He lost his title to Randy Turpin in 1951, retired in 1952, lost the title twice in 1957 to Gene Fullmer and Carmen Basilio, and lost it for the final time in 1960 to Paul Pender. As middleweight champion he was inconsistent. He only won eight out of the fifteen world middleweight title fights he had between 1951 and 1961. Ray was defeated by welterweight champion Carmen Basilio whereas Monzon knocked out welterweight champion Jose Napoles in a battle between champions.

Ray tended to cut easily, though he was never stopped in a fight due to cuts. Ray had a smooth style in the ring and his double left hook was quick and hard. Ray could box or punch and when he was up for a fight, he was nearly unbeatable. He was deadly when he had a fighter hurt, as evidenced in his second fight with Randy

Turpin in 1951. Badly cut Ray dropped Turpin in the 9th round and when he got up, Ray swarmed all over him with more than thirty punches before the referee stopped the fight.

Ray was a fan's delight to watch in the ring. He had blazing fast hand speed and he threw deadly combinations at opponents. His rope skipping exhibitions while he was in training drew large crowds. He had excellent footwork and quit the ring once to become a professional dancer.

A classic fight would have been between Ray, who, I believe, was regarded as the best middleweight in history in the second half of the 21st century, and Stanley Ketchel who was regarded as the best middleweight in the first half of the century. In this fight I believe that Ray would have been too slick for Ketchel and would have won a fifteen round decision over the wild swinging slugger. Unfortunately Ray, like many fighters, did not know when to retire and he probably stayed in the ring about five years too long. This probably tarnished his image somewhat.

Stanley Ketchel, I have listed as the 3rd best middleweight of all time. He and Bob Fitzsimmons were the two hardest punchers of all the middleweight champions. Ketchel was idolized by fellow fighters in the first half of the century because of his power, aggressive style of fighting, and his hard living outside of the ring. He was a hobo riding the rails across the country before he became a bouncer in a saloon in Butte, Montana.

He had knockout power and he was as dangerous in the 30th round of a fight as he was in the first. He had incredible stamina and tremendous courage as can be evidenced by the beating he took in his second fight with Billy Papke. He kept getting up until he was totally drained of his energy.

He had enough power to knock down heavyweight champion Jack Johnson before being knocked out. His style of fighting was total offense. If a middleweight stood in front of him and exchanged punches, his opponent was sure to get knocked out as no middleweight could take his punch.

Nat Fleisher, the founder of Ring magazine, listed Ketchel as the greatest middleweight champion of all time up until the 1950's. Although I think that Sugar Ray Robinson would have out boxed Ketchel, I feel that he had a chance of knocking out most of the top ten middleweights, with Monzon and Robinson being the exceptions.

Harry Greb, my 4th rated middleweight champion of all time, was a remarkable fighter who packed nearly 300 fights into a twelve year boxing career. He fought many of his fights blind in one eye. Harry would take on anybody, anywhere, at any time. He fought so often that he did not need to train between fights.

Harry is the only man to defeat heavyweight champion Gene Tunney and he spent most of his career beating the top middleweights, light heavyweights, and heavyweights of his day. He won the American light heavyweight championship in 1922 from Gene Tunney and the middleweight title from Johnny Wilson in 1923. He made six successful defenses of his title before losing it to Tiger Flowers on a split decision in 1926.

Harry had an all action awkward style of offense, which saw him throwing punches at all angles at opponents. Even though he did not have much of a punch, he had a solid chin inside of the ring. Some boxing experts rate Greb as the greatest middleweight of all time. His awkward offensive style may have been a problem for Monzon, Robininson, and Ketchel, but I do not see Harry beating those fighters rated above him here.

Bernard Hopkins is tied with Harry Greb for the 4th greatest middleweight champion of all time. Bernard holds most of the middleweight records, including having the most successful title defenses with twenty, and holding the middleweight title for the longest period of time, which was over ten years. Bernard was also the oldest man to ever hold the middleweight title.

Bernard also won the world light heavyweight championship and continued to fight at past fifty years of age. Bernard had a great defense and was an expert counterpuncher. He showed great ring control and an excellent sense of pace. He is truly a ring medical marvel, fighting and beating some of the top fighters in the game while past fifty years of age.

Though Bernard was hugely successful, I did not see him to be a particularly exciting fighter to watch in the ring. He was boringly effective and difficult to beat in the ring. I felt that Bernard was a modern day version of Charley Burley. I do not see Bernard beating any of the middleweights rated above him here, including Harry Greb, who he is tied with in 4th place.

Marvin Hagler holds down the 6th spot in the top ten of great middleweight champions. Marvelous Marvin was the best middleweight in the 1980's. It took him seven years to get a title fight and then Vito Antuofermo held him to a draw. When he finally won the title in 1980 from Alan Minter in London, the British threw bottles at him when he was in the ring.

He legally changed his name to Marvelous Marvin Hagler and held onto the title for seven years making title defenses against Antuofermo in a rematch and won a high profile fight against Tommy Hearns in 1985. He was a solid combination puncher with a granite chin. He took all of Tommy Hearns bombs without flinching and then came on to knock him out in the third round. He knocked out John "The Beast" Mugabi in a brutal slugfest and outfought Roberto Duran to win a close unanimous decision.

Marvin did have a problem with fast moving boxers such as Willie "The Worm" Monroe and Bobby "Boogaloo" Watts, a couple of Philadelphia fighters who won decisions from him in 1976. His biggest high profile fight was with Tommy Hearns until Sugar Ray Leonard decided to make a comeback and challenge Marvin for his middleweight title in 1987.

The Leonard fight was to be the highest profile fight of Marvin's career. Leonard had not fought in three years and had suffered a detached retina. Many boxing observers felt that the fight should not have even been made. Leonard demanded a twelve round fight instead of fifteen rounds and the Hagler camp agreed to this demand.

Leonard started off fast in the fight and won the first three rounds as Marvin just simply pursued without throwing any real punches. Marvin finally got into the fight around the 4th round and finished strong to make it close. Leonard, fighting in flurries, stole enough of the final rounds to gain a split decision victory. Marvin protested the decision but the real issue was how could a retired fighter like Leonard even come back after three years and put up such a good fight.

Leonard exposed Marvin's slowness of foot and would not give him a rematch. I personally scored Marvin's fight with Leonard 115-113 in favor of Leonard. I cannot see Marvin beating any of the five middleweight champions I've listed in front of him.

Marcel Cerdan is listed as number seven in the list of ten greatest middleweight champions. He was nicknamed "The Tiger of Casablanca" and many boxing experts think that he was the greatest French fighter of all time. He could box and he could punch. He had good defense and he was only stopped once in 114 fights. He had an amazing record of 111 wins, with just 4 losses. He won 65 fights by knockout.

Marcel learned to box in Casablanca and served in the French Army during the World War II years. After getting out of the army he continued his boxing career in France. He won the French middleweight title in 1945 and the European middleweight title in 1947.

Marcel invaded the United States rings in 1946 when he won a ten round decision over Georgie Abrams. He also defeated Anton Raadkik and knocked out Lavern Roach. Marcel lost his European title to Cyrille Delanoit in Brussels in May of 1948 but he regained the title in July by beating Delanoit with a fifteen round decision to set up his title fight with Tony Zale in September of 1948.

Marcel proved his greatness when he fought a perfectly paced fight to wear down the veteran Zale in the 12th round to win the world title. Marcel lost his title to LaMotta in June of 1949 when he injured his arm in the first round and fought one handed until he had to retire in his corner at the end of the 10th round.

Marcel died when his plane crashed in the Azores while flying back to the United States for the LaMotta rematch. Most boxing observers feel that Marcel would have probably defeated LaMotta in a rematch.

There is no doubt Marcel was a great fighter but, due to the circumstances, he did not get the opportunity to become a great champion. I could be rating Marcel too low in the number seven spot, but it is impossible to tell.

Former heavyweight, light heavyweight, and middleweight champion Bob Fitzsimmons is in the 8th spot of the greatest middleweight champions. Bob really needs no introduction to fight fans as he was the first man to become a champion in three different weight divisions.

Bob rarely weighted more than 165 pounds when he was knocking out heavyweights, and if he was fighting today, he would probably be fighting in the super middleweight limit of 168 pounds. Bob won the first of his titles in the middleweight division when he knocked out Jack "Nonpareil" Dempsey in 1891. He remained middleweight champion until around 1897 while only making one title defense during that time.

The middleweight limit around 1890 was around 154 pounds and Bob found it very difficult to make weight. Bob found, not only could he not make the middleweight fight limit anymore, but that there was no money to be made fighting in the middleweight division.

Bob was probably hardest puncher of all the top ten great middleweight champions and he would have always had a punchers chance of beating any of the other middleweight champions listed here.

The Man of Steel, Tony Zale occupies the number nine spot of great middleweight champions. Tony was a superbly conditioned fighter who came up from the ranks during the depression. He wore down his opponents with a relentless body attack. He was able to take all of middleweight champion Al Hostak's hardest punches in their three bout series and came back to knock him out in two of the fights and win a decision from him in the third fight.

Tony had great recuperative powers and even though he could be knocked down, it was difficult to put him down for the ten count. He was involved in some of the truly great wars in the ring. His three bout rivalry with Rocky Graziano was the most talked about in the middleweight division.

Tony seemed to get stronger even as he aged and came back from serving in the Navy in World War II. He showed the heart of a champion when he lost his title to Marcel Cerdan. Tony was truly a great middleweight and it is a pleasure to place him in the list of the ten greatest middleweight champions. I could honestly not see Tony beating any of the fighters ranked above him.

Nino Benvenuti completes the list of the top ten middleweight greats. I believe he was the best fighter to ever come out of Italy. He had an outstanding amateur career and was a super welterweight champion prior to becoming a two time middleweight champion in the 1960's.

He was a smooth boxer in the ring with quick hands and good lateral movement. His good looks and suave and debonair style in the ring made boxing fans of many women during his title reigns. As good a boxer as he was in the ring, he was no match for probably the best middleweight champion ever, Carlos Monzon. Monzon knocked him out and took his title in 1970 and made quick work of him in a rematch in 1971.

I believe he could be considered the best middleweight during the 1960's and deserves to be listed in the top ten great middleweight champions.

Honorable mention would include Jake LaMotta, Dick Tiger, and Joey Giardello. Though all three were great champions, I felt that they fell just short of being included in the top ten middleweight champions.

Carmen Basilio and Emile Griffith were not listed in this group because I would rate them as two of the greatest welterweight champions of all time. Basilio won the middleweight title from Robinson in 1957 but the majority of his title defenses were as the welterweight champion prior to the Robinson fight. Though Griffith won the middleweight title twice in the mid to late 1960's, he had already won the welterweight title three times in the earlier part of the decade.

SIX RING GREATS WHO NEVER GOT A SHOT AT THE TITLE

Due to the politics of boxing there were always fighters who deserved a shot at the title but never received one. Some of the fighters did not receive a title fight because of the politics of their country, such as Communism not allowing professional boxing. In other cases fighters did not receive a title fight because they were just too good and the champion did not want to risk losing his title. In some cases, especially near the early part of the 20th century, fighters were unable to get a title fight because of their color.

In other cases, boxing monopolies, like the International Boxing Club in the 1950's, made it virtually impossible for a fighter to get a title fight unless the fighter's manager was a member or was connected to the club. In several cases, it was just fate, as the World War II years cost many a fighter of a title fight as the titles were frozen during the peak fighting years of the war.

The following is a selection of fighters who fit in one of these categories and never got a title fight. The period covered of ring greats who did not receive a title bout was over a fifty year period from 1915 to 1965.

Les Darcy

Photograph from Ring Magazine, January 1977

Chapter Twelve   *Les Darcy*

The Australian Golden Boy

James Leslie Darcy was born on October 31, 1895, in New South Wales and fought under the name of Les Darcy. Your first reaction to this name would possibly be "who was he". The answer would be that he was probably the best middleweight in the world during the Great War years of 1914 to 1917, and may also be the greatest fighter to ever come out of Australia.

Les is still revered as a hero in Australia to this day and his is a story of triumph and tragedy. He was short for a middleweight, standing at about 5 foot 6 inches in height, and weighed between 147 and 160 pounds.

Les came from an impoverished family of twelve children and toiled on his family's farm. He became an apprentice black-smith which hardened his muscles, as the trade did for the three division world champion, Bob Fitzsimmons.

He turned professional after a short amateur career in 1910, at the age of 15, by winning an eleven round decision over George "Governor" Balser. A one round box off was needed to determine the winner of the fight.

In 1911, Les had but one fight when he won a four round decision over Tom Donahue under the management of Tom O'Sullivan. Les was undefeated in 23 fights with 14 wins coming by knockout. He suffered his first defeat when he lost a twenty round decision to Bob Whitelaw in a fight for the Australian welterweight title in November of 1913.

Les knocked out Whitelaw in a non-title rematch and had a record of 27 wins and 1 loss when he fought world ranked Fritz Holland in Sydney Stadium in Rushcutters Bay. Fighting in Sydney Stadium in Australia was equivalent to fighting in Madison Square Garden in New York.

Holland was managed by former heavyweight champion Tommy Burns and was a huge favorite in the fight. Both fighters stepped into the ring in July of 1914. Les came on strong over the last half of the fight but could not overcome Holland's early lead. The judges gave Holland the decision in the close fight.

A rematch with Holland took place in September. Les was giving Holland a boxing lesson and then dropped him in the 18th round with a body blow. Holland clutched his groin and claimed foul. The referee then proceeded to rule Holland the winner on a disqualification.

After three quick wins, Les was matched with Jeff Smith for the Australian version of the middleweight championship. In January of 1915, Smith went down in the 5th round claiming foul. Les was disqualified again for another alleged low blow. This was the last fight that Les would lose in his career.

In March of 1915, he decisioned old nemesis Fritz Holland in twenty rounds. In May Les gave Holland a rematch and knocked him out in the 13th round.

In May of 1915, Les again challenged Jeff Smith for the Australian version of the middleweight championship. In a strange quirk of fate, Les was awarded the title when he was fouled in the 2nd round by Smith. Les would successfully defend his middle weight title six times this year. His victims included world ranked fighters Eddie McGoorty, Mick King, Jimmy Clabby, Fred Dyer, and Billy Murray.

1916 was Les' best and last year in the ring. In February he knocked out Harold Hardwick in seven rounds to gain the Australian heavyweight title. Les defended his heavyweight title in March by knocking out Les O'Donnell. Les defended his middleweight title against Alex Costica in May and his heavyweight title, again, against Dave Smith, in August.

Les fought the greatest fights of his career in September. He successfully defended his middleweight title by decision against American Jimmy Clabby on the 9th and knocked out former middleweight champion George Chip on the 30th. Les won every round before knocking Chip out in the 9th round with a right to the jaw.

Les was a smooth boxer, who had power in both hands and incredible stamina. He had great reflexes and was considered "a natural" by everyone who had seen him fight. The legend of Les Darcy was growing in Australia as he beat the world's best middleweights and Australia's top heavyweights.

As good as Les was, he was not considered the world champion outside of Australia. The rest of the world considered Al McCoy of New York as the world champion. Les knew that he would have to travel to the United States and knock out McCoy to take the world title.

While Les was boxing in 1916, Australia was sending volunteers overseas to fight in the Great War. While there was no official draft, the local newspapers felt that it would be good for the soldier's morale if Les enlisted in the military. Since Australian men under the age of 21 needed parental consent to enlist in the military and Les was under 21 at the time, he needed his mother's permission to enlist but she refused.

American promoter Tex Rickard was in the process of lining up a series of fights for Les, including a title shot at world champion Al Coy, when the Australian government refused to issue him a passport.

Les was a confused youngster and he made a terrible mistake by leaving Australia illegally and stowing away on a tramp steamer to the United States in October of 1916. Les arrived on the American shores and the Australian press immediately labeled him a "slacker". The American newspapers picked up on the stories coming from the Australian press.

Les and Tex Rickard had underestimated the powers of the press when the Governor of New York denied Les a license to box and also termed him a "slacker". Other states followed in denying Les a license to box. Then the United States officially entered the Great War.

Les applied for United States citizenship and was eventually sworn in to the United States Army. Les was given a furlough to fight Len Rowlands of Milwaukee, Wisconsin. While training for the Rowlands fight in Memphis, Tennessee Les had some dental work done. His teeth became infected and he died from septicemia on May 24, 1917, at the age of 21.

Les' body was sent home to Australia where the same fickle fans who ostracized him for leaving the country during the time of war now welcomed him home, full of regret, as an Australian hero. Huge crowds lined the streets of Sydney for his funeral procession as the misunderstood and condemned youth was laid to rest. Forty years later a Les Darcy memorial was unveiled in his hometown of Maitland.

Les' final ring record was 46 wins and 4 losses. He won 29 fights by knockout. Les was fittingly inducted into the International Boxing Hall of Fame in 1993. How good was Les Darcy? He would have been good enough to knockout Al McCoy for the world middleweight championship in 1917.

Harry Wills

Photograph from Boxing Illustrated, April 1964

Chapter Thirteen   Harry Wills

The Black Panther

Harry Wills is the only heavyweight in my list of six who was never granted a title fight. He suffered from the after effects of the Johnson vs. Jeffries fight of 1910 in which racial riots occurred after the fight. Promoters were afraid to make a match between Jack Dempsey and Harry because of the racial issue and even more complex issues than just race alone.

Harry was born on May 15, 1892, in New Orleans, Louisiana, and turned professional in 1912. Harry grew to a height of 6 feet 2 inches and filled out to around 210-215 pounds. By 1913 he was fighting and beating top black fighters like Joe Jeanette. He had around seventeen fights with the legendary Sam Langford. He won the colored heavyweight championship three times from Langford. He took the titles from Langford in 1914, 1916, and 1918. He won the majority of his seventeen battles with Langford and achieved top heavyweight contender status when he knocked out Fred Fulton in 1920.

By 1920, Harry was challenging champion Jack Dempsey to a title bout, however Dempsey had other plans and they did not include defending his title against Harry. Dempsey chose a dying Billy Miske as his first opponent. He defended his title against the very ill Billy Miske in September, knocking him out in the third round. Dempsey was simply giving Miske a payday that he badly needed. In December Dempsey fought a top rated contender named Bill Brennan. Brennan was actually leading on the scorecards until Dempsey caught up to him in the 12th round and knocked him out.

Dempsey continued to ignore Harry's pleas for a title fight in 1921. Dempsey defended his title only once this year, knocking out light heavyweight champion Georges Carpentier. Harry maintained his status as the number one contender by knocking out contenders Gunboat Smith and Big Bill Tate.

In June of 1922, Dempsey actually signed a contract to fight Harry for the title. The promoter was supposed to be Tex Rickard and the fight was to take place in New York. The only problem was that the fight never took place. Apparently the powers to be in the New York boxing commission really did not want the fight and it was quite possible that Tex Rickard did not want the fight either.

Rickard had promoted the Jack Johnson vs. Jim Jeffries heavyweight title fight in 1910 and the result of that fight caused racial riots across the country. Dempsey was Rickard's meal ticket and he matched him very carefully in only big money fights.

Dempsey made two title defenses in 1923. He decisioned Tommy Gibbons in Shelby, Montana, on July 4th. The fight bankrupt the city due to the guaranteed monies paid to Dempsey. Dempsey won an uninspired fifteen round decision and did not come close to knocking Gibbons out.

Dempsey next defended against Luis Firpo who had recently knocked out a faded Jess Willard. In this famous fight, Dempsey was knocked out of the ring in a wild first round before he came back to knock Firpo out in the second round. Harry had sued to try and stop the Dempsey and Firpo fight but the fight took place anyway. Harry, again, found himself out in the cold.

In September of 1924, Harry accepted a high profile fight against the same Luis Firpo who had almost knocked out Dempsey the year before. Firpo looked slightly bigger than Harry in the ring and it was a highly anticipated match between the two sluggers.

Harry and Firpo both started off aggressively, but Harry was the sharper puncher and he dropped Firpo early in the fight. Firpo got up but it appeared that Harry did not really press this advantage. Harry won almost every round and won an easy newspaper decision.

Harry made another attempt to obtain a fight with Dempsey. This time both fighters agreed to a match and a promoter tried to hold the fight in Indiana. Negotiations fell through when Dempsey was not paid money due to him at the contract signing. This was the time when the fight should have taken place as both fighters were fading by 1926. Dempsey lost his title to Gene Tunney and Harry was thoroughly beaten before being disqualified against Jack Sharkey. Harry would eventually lose to Paulino Uzcudun in July of 1927, in his last high profile fight.

Several factors were in play as to why Harry never received a title fight. Obviously race was one of the issues. It did not appear that promoter Tex Rickard really wanted to promote the fight, nor did the New York Athletic Commission in 1922. In 1925, it appeared that the New York Athletic Commission was in favor of the fight but, apparently, the promoters could not come up with the guaranteed money required by Dempsey for the fight. Tex Rickard also defied the order of the New York State Athletic Commission that Dempsey must fight Wills or have his license suspended. Rickard simply moved the Dempsey versus Tunney fight to Philadelphia.

In my opinion the major roadblocks to the fight were the issue of race and Rickard's refusal to allow Dempsey to fight Wills. I do not believe that Dempsey was afraid of Wills but that Dempsey just allowed his managers and promotors decide who he fought. The public was ready for a Dempsey versus Wills match but the promoters at the time were not. In addition, the memory of Jack Johnson's behavior during his title reign still lingered over black fighters in the 1920's. Joe Louis was finally able to obtain a title fight in the 1930's which opened the doors for other black fighters to fight for the heavyweight title. Harry unfortunately just came along at the wrong time. He fought in the period between Jack Johnson and Joe Louis and this was unfortunate for Harry.

Did Harry Wills deserve a title fight during the 1920's? There is no doubt that Harry deserved to fight for the championship. Do I think that Harry Wills could have beaten Dempsey? Dempsey never had a problem fighting bigger men such as Jess Willard, Luis Firpo, or Fred Fulton. Harry was bigger than Dempsey but he could be hit. I believe that Dempsey punched too hard and fast for Harry and that Dempsey would have won a unanimous decision or stopped him in the late rounds of a fight.

Harry's final ring record was 71 wins, 9 losses, and 3 draws. He won 57 fights by knockout. Harry won 19 newspaper decisions and had 1 loss and 4 draws. Harry was inducted in the International Boxing Hall of Fame in 1992.

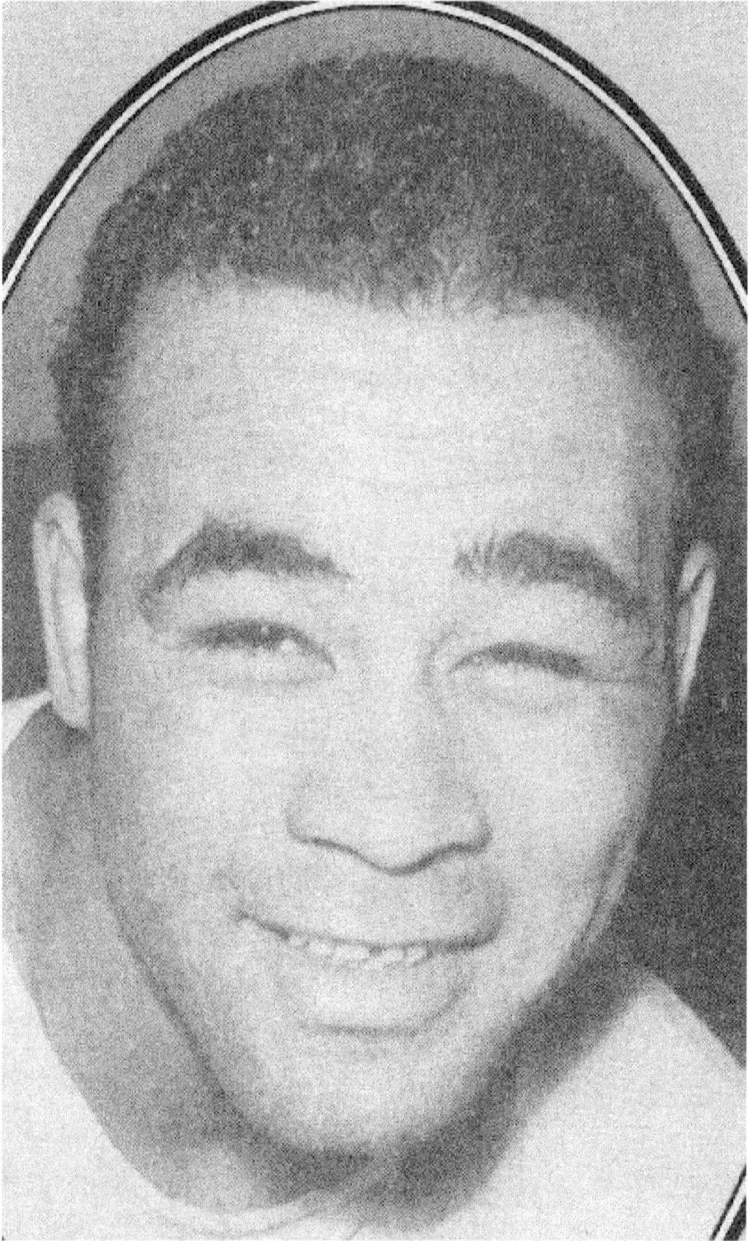

Charley Burley

Photograph from Boxing and Wrestling Magazine, September 1952

Chapter Fourteen   *Charley Burley*

The Uncrowned Champion

The term "Uncrowned Champion" was made famous by Charley Burley. Charley was a leading welterweight and middleweight contender in the 1940's. He was avoided by all the champions of his era including Henry Armstrong, Sugar Ray Robinson, Tony Zale, and Jake LaMotta.

He was born Charles Duane Burley on September 6, 1917, in Pittsburgh, Pennsylvania, to a black coal miner father and a white Irish immigrant mother. He began boxing in boy's clubs at the age of twelve in the Pittsburgh area and won several Golden Glove and Senior amateur championship titles.

In 1936 he refused to participate in the Olympic Trials as the Olympic Games were scheduled to be held in racist Nazi Germany. Charley opted to turn professional in 1936 and won his first twelve fights before he dropped a unanimous decision to Eddie Dolan in Pittsburgh in 1937.

Future welterweight champion Fritzie Zivic was one of the few top rated fighters who was not afraid to fight Charley. Charley lost a close split decision to Zivic in March of 1938. Charley won the rematch with Zivic by decision in June of the same year.

Unable to get a world title shot, Charley won the colored welterweight championship by unanimous decision over Cocoa Kid in August of 1938. Charley moved up to the middleweight division in November and won an easy decision over future middleweight champion Billy Soose.

Charley split a pair of decisions with Jimmy Leto in 1939 and won the rubber match with Fritzie Zivic in July. Moving back up to the middleweight division, Charley defeated Nate Bolden in February of 1940, and held top rated middleweight Georgie Abrams to a draw in July.

Charley won all eight of his fights in 1941 and defeated Holman Williams twice in 1942. His knockout victory in August over Williams earned him the world colored middleweight championship. Charley lost two close decisions to Ezzard Charles in 1942. There was no shame in losing to Ezzard Charles as he was nearly unbeatable at the time and he was a future world heavyweight champion.

Charley fought a heavyweight named J.D. Turner during the course of the year in a catch weight match. Outweighed by seventy pounds Charley totally dominated Turner before knocking him out in the 7th round.

Charley was at the top of his game in 1944. He traveled to California to win the state middleweight championship against Jack Chase on April 6th and, just two weeks later, he probably fought the best fight of his career when he challenged Archie Moore as a late substitute. Charley dropped Moore five times and won an easy unanimous decision against the Old Mongoose. Moore would later claim that Charley was one of the greatest fighters he ever saw.

Over the following years, Charley was unable to get a title fight and he had to be content with fighting other black fighters, known as "the black murderer's row", who were also denied title fights. He was still defeating top ranked fighters such as Oakland Billy Smith in the post war years but he was losing interest in the fight game.

Charley fought the last fight of his career in 1950 in Lima, Peru. He won a ten round decision over a fighter named Pilar Bastidas to close out his career. Charley needed to support his family as his boxing earnings dwindled. He worked as an aircraft mechanic and retired from the sanitation department in Pittsburgh.

Charley found no fame or glory during his boxing career, but he did get the respect of the boxing community. Like Archie Moore, veteran trainer Eddie Futch felt that Charley was one of the most complete fighters that he had ever seen.

The question is why did Charley never get a world title fight? Obviously the first reason is that he was such a good fighter that he was always a threat to take anybody's world title belt. Charley was avoided by all of the white and black champions of his day including Henry Armstrong and Sugar Ray Robinson. Welterweight champion Fritzie Zivic even went to the extent of buying Charley's contract to avoid fighting him.

The second reason is that Charley was in his prime during the World War II years from 1941 to 1945 when the world titles were frozen as a result of the champions serving in the military. The third reason is that the Tony Zale vs. Rocky Graziano trilogy denied other fighters an opportunity to challenge for the middleweight title between 1946 and 1948. The fourth reason may have been that, even though Charley was an expert boxer, he had a somewhat boring counterpunching style of fighting that made his opponents look bad and it did not make him a huge draw at the box office.

How would Charley have done against the world champions of his day? I believe he would have knocked out welterweight champion Freddie "Red" Cochrane but would have lost a decision to Sugar Ray Robinson. I believe Charley would have outpointed middleweight champion Rocky Graziano but lost a close decision to champion Tony Zale.

Charley ended up with a boxing record of 83 wins, 12 losses, and 2 draws and 1 no contest. He won 50 fights by knockout and was never knocked out. Charley was inducted into the International Boxing Hall of Fame in 1992.

Harry Matthews

Photograph from Boxing and Wrestling
Magazine, September 1952

Chapter Fifteen   Harry Matthews

The Kid

Can you name a professional fighter who was a top contender during the 1940's and 1950's and never got a title shot? Ok, let's make this easier to guess. This fighter was unbeaten in fifty-three fights over a nine year period from 1943 to 1952. Well, if you guessed Charley Burley, you are wrong. The fighter was Harry "Kid" Matthews.

Harry Matthews was born on December 9th, 1922, in Emmet, Idaho. After a few amateur fights and, after being encouraged by his father, he turned professional at the age of 14 in 1937. He became known as Harry "Kid" Matthews due to his young age.

Harry hooked up with manager George Blake from Los Angeles and fighting mostly out of Boise, Idaho, he went undefeated in his first sixteen professional contests. In his 17th professional fight, Harry met veteran middleweight Jackie Burke who had over one hundred professional fights. Harry lost his first professional fight and received a boxing lesson in the process.

Harry had developed a slick boxing style which made him hard to hit with a solid punch. Harry took his slick style of boxing with him to Seattle, Washington, in 1942, where he won a ten round majority decision over former middleweight world champion Al Hostak. Harry cracked the top ten in the middleweight rankings and a draw in a rematch with Hostak did nothing to hurt his status as a top contender. Unfortunately Harry went to California in 1943 where he lost two fights in a row to middleweight contenders Jack Chase and Eddie Booker. Harry lost his top ten ranking and joined the Army during the World War. Harry resumed his boxing career upon his discharge from the Army and in 1947 he won a decision over Paul Blanks for the Washington State middleweight championship.

In 1948, Harry won a decision over Jackie Burke in a rematch to avenge his earlier defeat. Harry also won the rubber match with Burke by knockout in 1949. After winning the rubber match with Burke, Harry hooked up with colorful fight promoter and manager, Jack Hurley. The first thing Hurley did was to teach Harry how to set down on his punching to create more power. Upon Hurley's urging Harry became more of a boxer-puncher, instead of being strictly a boxing stylist. The change in boxing style was made to increase Harry's gate appeal to bring in more money fights.

Harry moved up to the light heavyweight division and won a couple of small money fights in Omaha, Nebraska, in 1950. Harry closed out the year by winning a decision from tough Estonian, Anton Raadik, and then knocking him out in a rematch.

Hurley decided that it was time to move Harry up in competition and booked a fight for him in Madison Square Garden against top light heavyweight contender Irish Bob Murphy in March of 1951. Harry surprised Murphy, and the New York fight crowd, by winning an impressive ten round decision. Hurley showed no interest in trying to obtain a light heavyweight title fight for Harry against champion Joey Maxim, opting to try and go after the heavyweight championship instead.

Harry began his campaign to get a shot at the heavyweight title by knocking out Freddie Beshore in May of 1951, in Milwaukee, Wisconsin. In July of 1951, Harry defeated legendary black fighter Lloyd Marshall and beat tough ex-marine top contender Danny Nardico before the years end.

Jim Norris, president of the International Boxing Club, virtually controlled professional boxing in the 1950's. His club usually controlled who would be awarded any championship fights under his jurisdiction. Hurley had a great relationship with the country's sports writers and he claimed that Harry was being blocked from getting any chances at big money fights by Norris and his group. Hurley even complained to the United States Congress about Harry being blacklisted from any title fights.

Harry was finally allowed to participate in a big money fight with top rated heavyweight Rex Layne in May of 1952 in Portland, Oregon. Harry was too fast for the slow footed Layne and walked away with the decision.Hurley began using the press to build Harry up as a legitimate heavyweight contender and claimed that his fighter could no longer make the light heavyweight limit.

Harry was given the chance to fight top heavyweight Rocky Marciano in a title eliminator fight with the winner to get a shot at heavyweight champion Joe Walcott. Curley did a great job of promoting Harry for the title eliminator fight but the truth was that Harry was still a legitimate light heavyweight and was no match for Marciano, strength wise.

The title eliminator match with Marciano was set for July of 1952 inside of Yankee Stadium in New York. Harry started out fast in the first round. He appeared too quick for Marciano and made him look clumsy at times during the round. The second round was a carbon copy of the first round until Marciano landed a series of left hooks to the jaw that dropped Harry on his back in a corner of the ring. At the count of ten Harry was still on his hands and knees hanging half way outside of the ropes trying to get up. The fight was over and Harry's dreams of fighting for the heavyweight championship ended with the Marciano fight.

Harry beat Freddie Beshore twice in 1953 but then he lost three straight fights to British heavyweight contender Don Cockell. Harry defeated former heavyweight champion Ezzard Charles in 1956 when Charles was past his prime. Harry would finish his career as a winner when he defeated Alvin Williams in November of 1956 in Boise, Idaho.

The question is why Harry never got a title fight in any weight division? He was certainly good enough to fight for a title; therefore there must have been other reasons for failing to get a title match.

Harry turned professional in 1937 and by 1942 he was beating top middleweight contenders. Unfortunately he lost his last two fights before entering the Army and did not begin fighting again until 1946 when Tony Zale and Rocky Graziano started trilogy of fights for the middleweight title.

Harry teamed up with Jack Hurley in 1949 and Hurley changed his style of fighting. He did obtain big money fights for Harry with Irish Bob Murphy and Rocky Marciano. I feel that Hurley made a huge mistake by not taking a title fight offer from light heavyweight champion Joey Maxim. I believe Harry had a good chance to take the title from Maxim and then, as light heavyweight champion, challenge Joe Walcott for the heavyweight title without having to face Marciano. Realistically Harry was just a light heavyweight and Marciano was a two fisted terror who nobody ever beat. Hurley's gamble to go after the heavyweight title, and not the light heavyweight title, cost Harry a shot at any title which he so richly deserved after twenty years of fighting with over one hundred fights.

Harry retired to Everett, Washington, where he owned a bar and welding shop before he passed away at the age of 80 in 2003. Harry's final ring record was 90 wins, 7 losses, 6 draws, and 1 no contest. He had 61 wins by knockout. Sadly, rarely is his name ever

mentioned for consideration for the International Boxing Hall of
Fame.

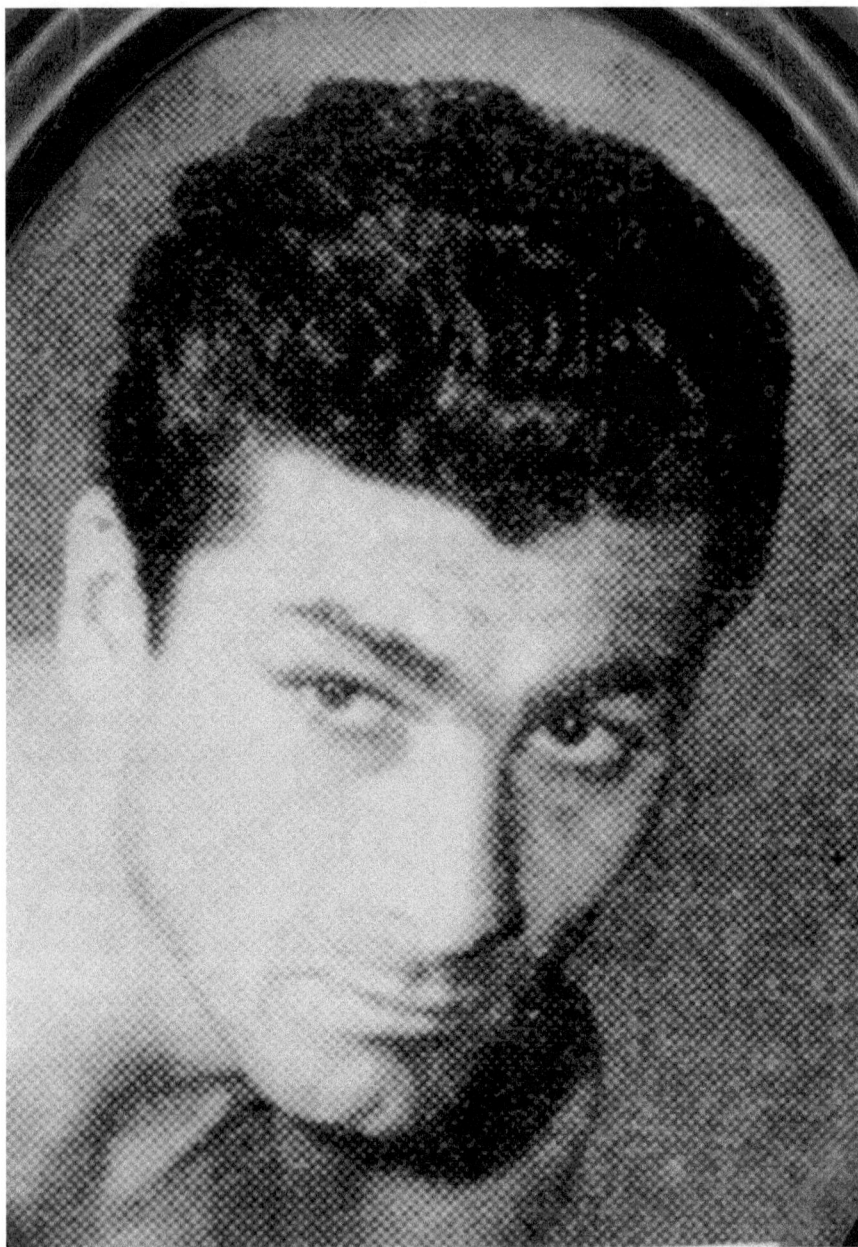

Eduardo Lausse

Photograph from Ring Magazine, February 1956

Chapter Sixteen   Eduardo Lausse

The Argentine Strongman

Before there was Carlos Monzon, there was Eduardo Lausse. He flashed across the United States television screens in the 1950's like a meteor. He left, made a brief appearance in 1960, and then he was gone forever. Who was this man? And why did he never fight for a world title? He was born Eduardo Jorge Lausse on November 27, 1927, in Buenos Aires, Argentina.

Eduardo turned professional in 1947 and quickly plowed through his competition with his devastating left hook. He immediately cleaned out the South American competition and was then matched with current welterweight champion Kid Gavilan in a non-title fight. Eduardo rocked Gavilan on several occasions but Gavilan's experience was the difference in the fight and Gavilan walked off with a close decision.

Eduardo caught the eye of famed boxing manager Charley Johnston on one of his tours of South America with light heavyweight champion Archie Moore. Johnston brought Eduardo to the United States in 1953 to fight in White Plains, New York. Eduardo knocked out Johnny Darby in February and Gus Mell in March. In April, Eduardo traveled to Providence, Rhode Island, where he knocked out Tommy Smith. He then returned to Argentina to win the Argentine middleweight title in July by knocking out Mario Diaz.

Eduardo returned to the United States in 1954 and won fights by knockout in a couple of New York's smaller clubs. The main body of the New York boxing public got their first look at the heavy handed Argentine middleweight with the deadly left hook in June when he fought Joe Rindone in Madison Square Garden. Eduardo destroyed Rindone with his knockout power and the New York boxing public could not get enough of watching him fight.

Instead of taking more fights in the United States, Eduardo headed back to Argentina to fight. He would get homesick in the United States and Johnston could not keep him there long enough to sufficiently promote him for a title fight.

Johnston enticed Eduardo back to Madison Square Garden in May of 1955 to defeat top contender Ralph "Tiger" Jones by a bloody ten round decision. Eduardo was cut around the eyes in this fight and cuts would continue to be a problem in his boxing career. He, next, returned to Buenos Aires in September to fight Kid Gavilan in a rematch. Eduardo outmuscled and outfought Gavilan to win a twelve round decision.

Eduardo took on future middleweight champion Gene Fullmer next in Madison Square Garden. He dropped Fullmer in the 8th round and won a hard fought unanimous decision in the battle between the two sluggers.

Johnston began making offers to middleweight champion Carl "Bobo" Olson to defend his title against Eduardo in Buenos Aires. Olson chose instead to go after Archie Moore's light heavyweight title and to defend his middleweight title against Robinson at the years end. Olson was knocked out in both fights.

Unable to land an immediate title fight, Eduardo took on middleweight contender Bobby Boyd in Chicago, in February of 1956. Eduardo dropped Boyd in the fight, but suffered a severe eye cut due to a head butt. Eduardo fought through a mask of blood but, in a very close fight, Boyd won a split decision. Eduardo was enraged by what he felt was a gift decision by the Chicago officials.

Instead of staying in the United States and trying to fight his way back to top contender status, he hopped on a plane and headed back to South America again. In June of 1956, he knocked out Humberto Loayza in Buenos Aires, to win the South American middleweight title. Eduardo stayed in South America and lost his South American middleweight title to Andres Selpa. In a three bout series, Eduardo finally defeated Selpa by decision in their 3rd fight.

Charley Johnston was finally able to convince Eduardo to return to the United States for one final run at the middleweight title. Eduardo took on Wilf Greaves in March of 1960, at Madison Square Garden. He knocked Greaves out in impressive fashion and Johnson began trying to arrange a title fight with either Paul Pender or Gene Fullmer.

Eduardo took a tune up fight with muscular Frenchman Marcel Pigou in St. Nicks arena in New York. Eduardo came out aggressively and was on the verge of stopping Pigou in the 5th round when the bell rang to end the round. Eduardo was dropped in the 7th round and took a short count. He got up and was defending himself when referee Arthur Mercante stepped in and stopped the fight. Everyone in the arena was surprised by the quick stoppage and Eduardo was off again to Argentina, never to return.

In Argentina, Eduardo had one final fight. He stopped Victor Salazar in November and then retired from the ring. Eduardo retired financially secure with his ring earnings and opened up several businesses in Argentina. He retired as a boxing hero in Argentina and was loved by all the fight fans.

So why did Eduardo never get a title fight? One reason is because he never stayed in the United States long enough to be properly promoted for a title fight by Charley Johnston. Boxing in the 1950's was controlled by Jim Norris and his International Boxing Club. If you were not connected to this promotional organization, you were not going to get a title fight. The only title fights in 1955 and 1956 were between Sugar Ray Robinson and Carl "Bobo" Olson. Another problem was that Eduardo lost key fights to Bobby Boyd in 1956 and Marcel Pigou in 1960, when he was on the verge of a title fight. The fight with Boyd was close and the decision could have gone either way and, with his fight with Pigou, he was a victim of an early stoppage by the referee.

How would Eduardo have done against the middleweight champions of his day? He had already decisioned Gene Fullmer in 1955 and, I believe, he would have knocked out Carl "Bobo" Olson in a title fight. I believe he would have lost a decision to Sugar Ray Robinson or been stopped by cuts in the late rounds.

Eduardo, like Harry Matthews, is not in the International Boxing Hall of Fame. I believe Eduardo along with Matthews, should be given strong consideration to be enshrined into this select group. Eduardo most assuredly would have won one of the alphabet middleweight titles of today. His final ring record was 75 wins, 10 losses, and 2 draws. He won 62 fights by knockout.

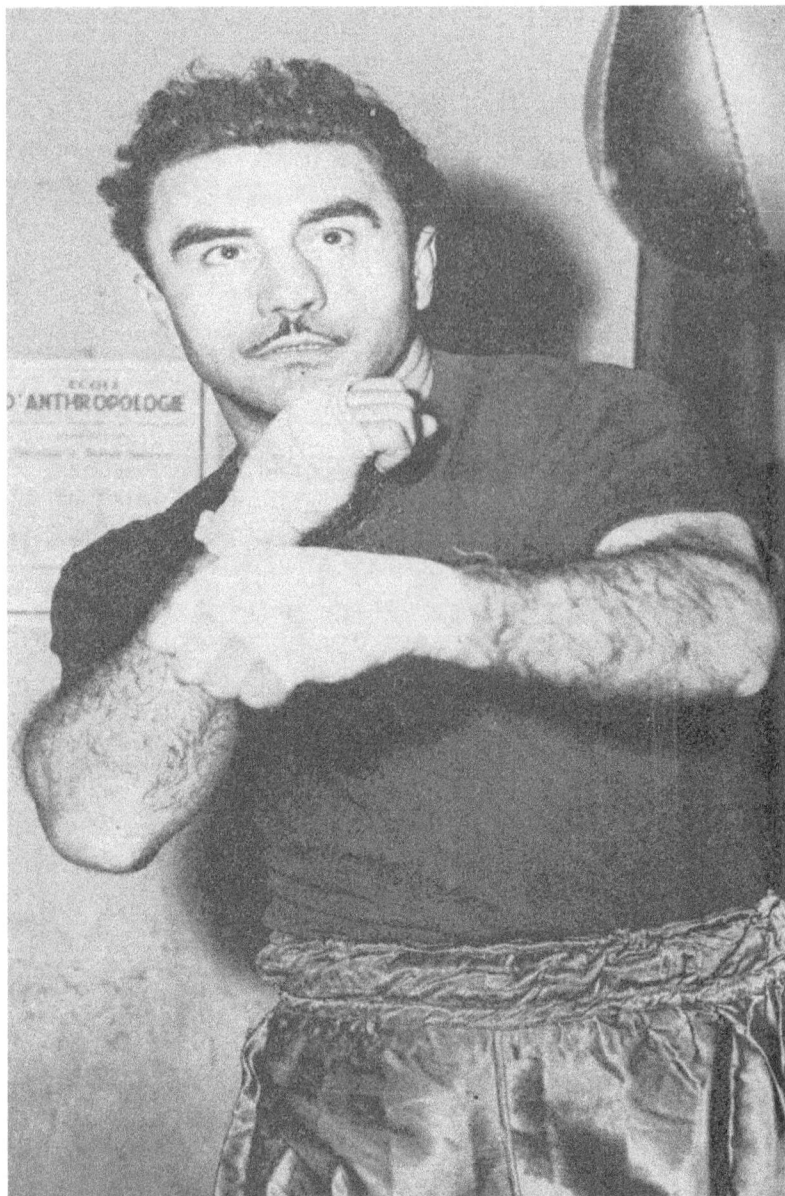

Laszlo Papp

Photograph from Boxing and Wrestling Magazine, November 1964

Chapter Seventeen   *Laszlo Papp*

Behind the Iron Curtain

Laszlo Papp was one of the most decorated amateur boxers in the history of the Olympic Games. He won Gold Medals in the light middleweight and middleweight divisions in 1948, 1952, and 1956. The Hungarian southpaw dominated his Olympic foes with his southpaw stance, vicious left hook, and vast amateur experience.

Laszlo Papp was born on March 25, 1926, in Communist Budapest, Hungary. He grew to be 5 foot 5 inches tall and weighed around 155 to 165 pounds when competing in the Olympics. By 1948 Olympic Games in London he was already an experienced amateur boxer who totally dominated his competition to take the Olympic Gold medal in the middleweight division.

Laszlo captured the European amateur middleweight championship in Oslo, Norway, in 1949, and dropped down to the light middleweight limit to capture his second Olympic Gold Medal in the 1952 Helsinki, Finland, Olympic Games. At the age of 30, Laszlo won his record breaking third Olympic Gold Medal in the light middleweight division in the 1956 Melbourne, Australia, Olympic Games. Laszlo returned to Hungary an Olympic Games hero.

Most boxers of today would have turned professional after boxing in just one Olympic Game, but due to the fact that professional boxing was banned in Hungary, he had to remain an amateur boxer. After a record of around 300 amateur wins and just 12 losses, Laszlo turned professional in 1957. Because of the ban on professional boxing, he traveled to Austria to train and fight.

Laszlo was 31 years old when he turned professional and had a history of fighting with brittle hands. Fighting infrequently due to training issues and to injured hands, he still won his first seven professional fights and then was held to a draw by the very ordinary Germinal Ballarin in April of 1959. Laszlo racked up a few more wins before he was held to another questionable draw by Giancarlo Garbelli in December of 1960. Laszlo did not look sharp in the Garbelli fight and some critics wondered if his best days in boxing were behind him.

Laszlo decided to continue his career and a ten round decision win over faded American middleweight Ralph "Tiger" Jones led to a challenge for the European middleweight title against Chris Christensen in May of 1962. In the best performance of his professional career, Laszlo knocked out Christensen to win the European title. Laszlo traveled across Europe to successfully defend his title on six occasions. He defended his title in Germany, France, Spain, Italy, Denmark, and Austria. Laszlo was a true road warrior when it came to defending his European crown. His more well-known defenses were against Harry Scott, Luis Folledo, and Mick Leahy.

After Laszlo knocked out Christensen in a European title rematch in July of 1964, he began clamoring for a world title fight with middleweight champion Joey Giardello. He took a tune up fight before his title challenge when he successfully defended his European title against Mick Leahy in October of 1964. The Hungarian government then refused to issue Laszlo a travel visa after the Leahy fight and his hopes for a title fight ended. It was felt that Hungary's Communist government was jealous of his popularity and decided to put an end to his professional career.

In analyzing the career of Laszlo Papp, there is no doubt that he may have been one of the greatest boxers in the history of the Olympic Games. When Laszlo turned professional he was already 31 years of age and a veteran of over 300 amateur fights. One would have to wonder if he was past his prime as a professional. The cagey Hungarian southpaw, with the vicious left hook, still had a somewhat limited, but successful professional career. He won the European middleweight championship and was certainly a top ten fighter in the middleweight division. It is incredible that turning professional at an advanced age with brittle hands, and poor training facilities he was still able to remain undefeated and qualify for a title fight.

I believe if Laszlo had turned professional after the 1948 Olympic Games, he would have eventually had to face Sugar Ray Robinson in the early 1950's to win the title. I do not believe that Laszlo could have defeated Robinson. I also suspect in a battle of two veterans, that Giardello would have won a decision over Laszlo in 1964. The politics of the day certainly disrupted Laszlo's professional career and it truly was a shame that he did not at least get to have a chance at the middleweight title.

Laszlo was inducted into the International Boxing Hall of Fame in 2001. I do not necessarily agree that he should have been inducted into this Hall of Fame if an induction is based solely on one's professional boxing career. There is no doubt that Laszlo belongs in an amateur boxing hall of fame.

Upon his retirement Laszlo remained active in sports and coached the Hungarian national amateur boxing team for over 20 years. Laszlo is still revered today as a hero in his native Hungary. A sports arena is named after him in his hometown of Budapest.

Laszlo's final ring record was 27 wins and 2 draws. He won 15 fights by knockout and retired undefeated as a professional. Laszlo passed away in his hometown in Hungary in 2003.

Bibliography

Information from the following publications was used in preparation for this book:

The Ring magazine, May of 1940 issue

The Ring Magazine, December of 1948 issue

The Ring Magazine, April of 1953 issue

The Ring Magazine, June of 1988 issue

Boxing's Greatest Middleweights by S. De Cristofaro, 1982

The Legendary Champions, by Rex Lardner, 1972

Sugar Ray, by Sugar Ray Robinson with Dave Anderson, 1969

World Boxing Magazine, November 1976 issue

Boxing Scene magazine, January 1990 issue

Boxing and Wrestling Magazine, May 1954 issue

The Killings of Stanley Ketchel, by James Carlos Blake, 2006

Acknowledgments

This book would not have been possible without the help and guidance of the following people:

Dean E. Lingenfelter, Editor

David R. Williams, Technical Support

Don Cogswell, President of the I.B.R.O.

Dan Cuoco, Vice President of the I.B.R.O.

Bill Paxton, Author of "The Fearless Harry Greb"

John Sheppard, of BoxRec

Luckett Davis, Box Rec stats

Herb Goldman, Box Rec stats

About the Author

The author, Larry Carli, is a retired Sheriff Detective and District Attorney Criminal Investigator from Sacramento County, California. He has published one book titled "The Illinois Thunderbolt", the life story of boxer Billy Papke, and has written freelance boxing stories for Boxing Illustrated, Fight Beat, and the Ring magazines.

The author is also a proud member of the International Boxing Research Organization, the National Sportscasters and Sportswriters Association, and the California Writers Club.

www.ingramcontent.com/pod-product-compliance
Lightning Source LLC
LaVergne TN
LVHW021505080426
835509LV00018B/2403